EQUIVALENTS

3 tsp. = 1 Tbsp.
4 Tbsp. = ¼ cup
5⅓ Tbsp. = ⅓ cup
8 Tbsp. = ½ cup
16 Tbsp. = 1 cup
1 cup = 8 oz.
1 cup = ½ pint
2 cups = 1 pint
4 cups = 1 quart
4 quarts = 1 gallon
16 ounces = 1 pound

# HEART
## OF THE
### HOME

If in your house
this book you see
Please hurry!
Bring it back to me. ♥

"Go, little book, and wish to all
Flowers in the garden, meat in the hall,
A bin of wine, a spice of wit,
A house with lawns enclosing it,
A living river by the door,
A nightingale in the sycamore!"

♥ Robert Louis Stevenson ♥

# HEART OF THE HOME

## NOTES FROM A VINEYARD KITCHEN

### 30th Anniversary Edition

BY SUSAN BRANCH

SPRING STREET Publishing

MARTHA'S VINEYARD · MASSACHUSETTS

Spring Street Publishing
P O  B O X  2 4 6 3
VINEYARD HAVEN, MA
0 2 5 6 8
sales@springstreetpublishing.com

SECOND EDITION
ISBN 978-0-9960440-3-5

Library of Congress Control Number
2016904139

♥ Excerpt from "He Digs, He Dug, He Has Dug" by Ogden Nash reprinted by permission of Little, Brown and Company from Verses From 1929 On. Copyright 1949 by Ogden Nash.
♥ Caption from cartoon by E.B. White and Carl Rose reprinted by permission of The New Yorker. Copyright 1928, 1956 The New Yorker Magazine, Inc.
♥ Excerpt from Mainstays of Maine by Robert P. Tristram Coffin reprinted by permission of author's heirs. Copyright 1944 by The Macmillan Company.

10 9 8 7 6 5 4 3 2 1

RRD-OH  ♥ ♥ ♥

PRINTED IN THE
UNITED STATES OF AMERICA

# DEDICATION

There is nothing like a big family ⁓ I know because I am the oldest of eight children & I feel very lucky for it ⁓ we have more fun, more stories & more memories & forever we'll hang together. ♥ This book is dedicated to them: to my Grandma, who has always been the heart of our home; to my Dad, Jack, who worked so hard to make our life good & whose laugh we love to hear; to my Mom, Pat, who is pure sunshine & loved her little "dolls" so well; and to my brothers and sisters ⁓ the singingest, dancingest, funniest and happiest bunch of maniacs I know: Tim, Steve, Chuck, Brad, Paula, Mary and Shelly. ♥ I love you all. ♥

For Tim ♥

♥ The Poppy is the California State Wildflower ♥

# HOME-BORN HAPPINESS

**B**ack in 1986, when HEART of the HOME was first published, I never imagined that 30 years later I'd be working on an "anniversary edition." Hand writing & painting 🎨 new pages for this book was like going back in time, remembering life in my first little house on the Island 🏠 in the old days before balsamic vinegar & artisan bread were staples at the 🏠 supermarket.

**T**he 1980s were an amazing time for cooking ~ new ingredients were being introduced every day, & there were no food police. We could still drink cream if we wanted to. Since then, it's been fat free, sugar free, carb free, meat free, dairy free, nut free, & gluten free. This book doesn't know from any of that. This book thinks food is LOVE. I tried to tell it, but surprise! Turns out, she's a fairy tale girl. 💜 (Not to mention, a step-granddaughter of Julia Child. 💜)

**S**o I decided not to "modernize" & let her be what she originally was, a country cookbook full of easy, homey, classic recipes, good enough for company. I wanted her to keep her time in cooking history 🪣, so that young cooks can see how hard we had it back then, the awesomeness 🪣 of our "back to the garden" generation, making our own hummus & pesto from scratch. 👧 WOW I'm just sayin'.

**Y**es, things have changed, but one thing is forever ~ & that's the feeling we get when we come in from the cold to a warm kitchen filled with the fragrance of baking brownies or simmering chicken stock, a feast for the senses that spells H·O·M·E. HEART of the HOME is a collection of recipes I've used all my life. It was a joy to do this, like making all new clothes for your very best doll. 💜 It's also tangible proof that dreams do come true. 💜

With L♥VE from the Heart of the Home & me... Susan Branch

I know I chatter on far too much...but if you only knew
how many things I want to say & don't. Give me
SOME credit. ♥ L.M. Montgomery

Go. Be. Love. The world needs you. ♡

# CONTENTS

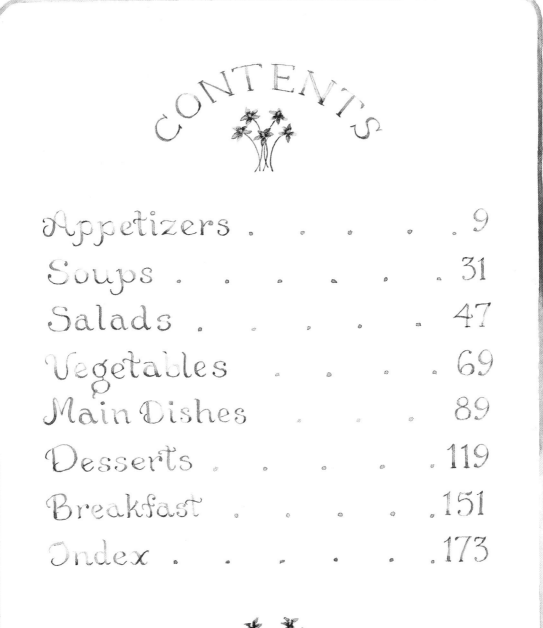

"To Adam Paradise was home.
To the good among his descendants
home is paradise."

Hare

# APPETIZERS

"To invite a person into your house is to take charge of his happiness for as long as he is under your roof." A. Brillat-Savarin ～

# APPETIZER IDEAS

- Scoop out cherry tomatoes with melon-baller and fill with pesto, p. 81.

- Lay out slices of ham and spread with softened cream cheese with chives. Roll up and slice. Chill.

- Put cream cheese with chives on a Bremner wafer. Top with a fat slice of radish.

- Wrap seedless grapes with a mixture of cream cheese and Roquefort cheese. Roll in chopped nuts. Chill.

- Mix cream cheese with chives, and minced parsley, with chopped red pepper. Spread on toasted cocktail rye bread.

## CHICKEN WINGS
YUM 325°   24 pieces

24 chicken "drumettes"
½ c. honey
2 Tbsp. Worcestershire sauce

⅓ c. soy sauce
1 clove garlic, minced
Juice of 2 lemons

If your market does not sell the "drumettes", buy a package of 12 chicken wings, remove the wing tips, and break each into two pieces. Preheat oven to 325°. Put the wings into a shallow baking dish. Mix remaining ingredients and pour over. Bake for 1 hour and serve warm.

# NEW POTATOES

2 dozen tiniest new potatoes
1/2 c. sour cream
chopped chives
crumbled bacon (or caviar)

Cook the potatoes. Cut each in half and scoop out a small cavity
with a melon-baller. Fill with sour cream, chives and bacon. ♥

# ARTICHOKE DIP

Mix together:
1 jar artichoke hearts ~ drained and chopped
1 c. mayonnaise
1 c. Parmesan cheese

Bake at 350° for 30 minutes. Serve with hot French bread or pita. ♥

# CHEESE BITES

Toast rounds of bread on one side and let cool. Mix together
1/2 c. mayonnaise, 1/2 c. Parmesan cheese and 1/4 c. minced onion.
Spread mixture on untoasted side of bread and broil till
brown and bubbly. Serve hot. ♥

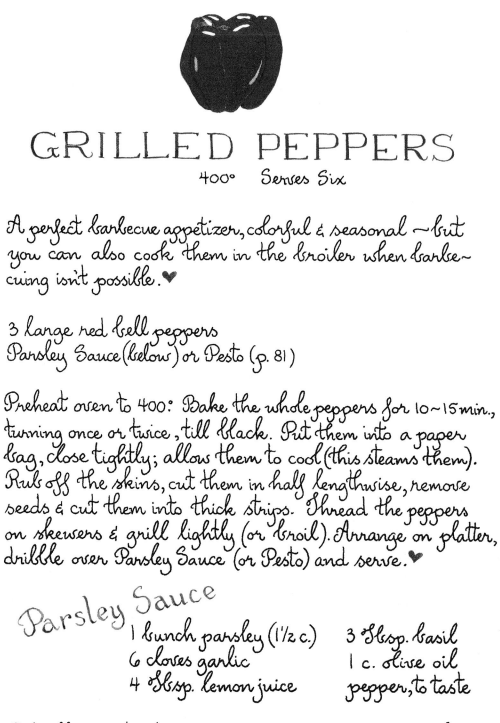

# GRILLED PEPPERS
400°   Serves Six

A perfect barbecue appetizer, colorful & seasonal — but you can also cook them in the broiler when barbe~ cuing isn't possible. ♥

3 large red bell peppers
Parsley Sauce (below) or Pesto (p. 81)

Preheat oven to 400° Bake the whole peppers for 10~15 min., turning once or twice, till black. Put them into a paper bag, close tightly; allow them to cool (this steams them). Rub off the skins, cut them in half lengthwise, remove seeds & cut them into thick strips. Thread the peppers on skewers & grill lightly (or broil). Arrange on platter, dribble over Parsley Sauce (or Pesto) and serve. ♥

## Parsley Sauce

1 bunch parsley (1½ c.)          3 Tbsp. basil
6 cloves garlic                  1 c. olive oil
4 Tbsp. lemon juice              pepper, to taste

Put all ingredients in food processor & purée. ♥ This sauce is also delicious on pasta. ♥

12

# STEAMED CHINESE DUMPLINGS

### Makes 20

You can serve these as hors d'oeuvres or alongside a salad for the first course of a Chinese dinner. ♥

2 Tubes refrigerated dinner rolls
1 lb. ground pork
4 Tbsp. minced green onion
3 Tbsp. soy sauce
1 Tbsp. sesame oil
½ c. chopped water chestnuts
freshly ground pepper
½ tsp. salt

Lay dinner rolls on lightly floured board ~ flatten with palm of hand then roll out with floured rolling pin till about 4" in diameter. Mix all other ingredients well. Put about 1½~2 Tbsp. pork mixture in the center of each round ~ gather up sides to meet in middle ~ twist top to close tightly. Put a damp cloth in the top part of vegetable steamer & put the dumplings on the cloth, 1" apart. Steam over boiling water for 20 min. Serve. ♥

# FRIED BRIE

Serves Six

This would also be wonderful served in a light lunch with cold Stuffed Artichokes (p.57). ♥ Try crisp, tart apple slices as an accompaniment to the cheese. ♥

½ c. milk
2 Tbsp. heavy cream
1 lg. egg
½ wheel Brie cheese, chilled
3½ c. French bread crumbs, finely ground

1 tsp. coarsely ground pepper
1 Tbsp. minced parsley
⅛ tsp. thyme
Oil

Combine milk, cream & egg. Remove rind from Brie and cut into 6 slices. Dip each piece into milk mixture, and then coat thickly with bread crumbs, pepper, parsley & thyme (mixed together). Refrigerate coated cheese for 15 minutes. Remove from refrigerator, dip again in milk mixture, & coat once more with crumbs. Heat 2" oil in a large skillet over moderately high heat. Fry for a few seconds, till brown and crisp on both sides. Serve ♥.

"You two can be what you like, but since I am the big fromage in this family, I prefer to think of myself as the Gorgon Zola."

Ogden Nash ♥

# CARPACCIO

Makes about 45

Don't be put off by the raw beef ~ this is an exciting hors d'oeuvre that will be snapped up in a second. ♥ Its imperative that you (or the butcher) slice the meat paper-thin; its easier if its partially frozen. ♥

- ♥ 1¼ lbs. very lean top round steak
  Slice paper-thin
- ♥ 3 French bread baguettes
  Slice the bread in ¼" slices. Put them in a single layer on a cookie sheet & bake at 275° for 10 min. until dry. Cool & reserve.
- ♥ Tarragon Butter
  1 c. butter, softened
  2 Tbsp. tarragon, minced
  3 Tbsp. parsley, minced
  1 Tbsp. fresh lemon juice
  Cream all ingredients together & refrigerate.
- ♥ Carpaccio Sauce
  4 Tbsp. red onion, chopped
  3 garlic cloves
  1 c. parsley, chopped
  4 anchovy filets
  10 cornichons (tiny French pickles)
  ½ c. capers
  5 Tbsp. Dijon mustard
  ¼ c. vinegar
  2 Tbsp. fresh lime juice
  1 tsp. Worcestershire sauce
  ¼ c. olive oil
  ¼ c. vegetable oil
  Put all ingredients except oil into food processor; whirl 20 seconds. Combine the olive & vegetable oils; with machine running, add oil in a very slow steady stream until thickened. Cover & refrigerate.
- ♥ To Serve
  Butter the bread. Cover each slice with a thin piece of meat & top with a little sauce. ♥

# CLAMS CASINO

450° Makes 1 dozen

Serve these with heated French bread for mopping up the garlic butter. ♥

1 doz. littleneck clams
4 Tbsp. garlic butter (recipe below)
4 Tbsp. red pepper, minced
4 slices bacon, partially cooked
3 Tbsp. bread crumbs
3 Tbsp. Parmesan cheese, grated

Preheat oven to 450°. Open clams; loosen meat from both top & bottom & pour off liquid. Make garlic butter. Cook bacon till almost done but still soft; cut into 1" pieces. On each clam, put a tsp. of garlic butter, a tsp. of red pepper, a piece of bacon, & cover with a mixture of bread crumbs & grated Parmesan. Bake on a cookie sheet for 10 min. till browned. Serve with lemon wedges. ♥

# GARLIC BUTTER

Cream together: ½ c. butter, 2 cloves minced garlic, ¼ c. minced shallots, ¼ c. minced parsley, 2 Tbsp. lemon juice, & 2 Tbsp. white wine (opt.). ♥

♥ Helpful hint: Push cloves of garlic into ground near base of rose bushes & raspberries ～ helps to deter pests & improve growth. ♥

# GUACAMOLE

Use only the bumpy, thick-skinned avocados. The smooth, thin-skinned ones are watery and have very little flavor. ♥

2 avocados, mashed                    1 tsp. salt
1 Tbsp. grated onion                  1/4 tsp. chili powder
1 Tbsp. fresh lemon juice             1 diced tomato

Mash avocados with potato masher. Add all other ingredients and mix well. Serve with tortilla chips or with Quesadillas. ♥

# QUESADILLAS

Melt a pat of butter in a large skillet. Lay a flour tortilla in the pan and cover it with thinly sliced jack cheese. Put another tortilla on top of the cheese. Cover the pan and cook over low heat until cheese is almost melted. Flip the tortilla over and brown the other side. Cut it like a pie and serve with sour cream and/or salsa. ♥ I like to put chopped mild green chili peppers in with the cheese, or if you like it hot, try it with sliced jalapeño peppers. Yum. ♥

♥  ♥  ♥  ♥  ♥

"Many's the long night I've dreamed of cheese —
     toasted mostly."
                    ♥ Robert Louis Stevenson ♥

# S U S H I

Makes 2 rolls & 6 rice cakes

Sushi is easy to make ~ in fact, after the first time you probably won't need a recipe. Also, I will give you just a couple of ideas for fillings, but you will see that your imagination is the only limit. The ingredients are avail~ able at health food stores and gourmet food shops. ♥

1 pkg. sushi nori (edible seaweed)
1 c. short grain white rice, uncooked
¼ c. rice vinegar
1 Tbsp. sugar
1 pkg. wasabi powder
1 pkg. pickled ginger
soy sauce
2 stalks celery
2 carrots
1 cucumber
6 large shrimp

Sushi platter suggestion ~ chives for stems ~ sushi for flowers. ♥

You'll also need long wooden picks & a "su", a bamboo sushi mat.

Cook the rice. Cut celery & carrots into thin strips. Peel, seed, & quarter the cucumber. Vegetables should be very fresh & crisp. In a tiny cup, mix 1 Tbsp. wasabi powder with just enough water to make a thick paste. Turn the cup upside-down on the counter to "set-up" (about 10 min.) Mix together the vinegar & the sugar. Stir the mixture into the cooked rice. Cool the rice slightly. Take one sheet of nori, lay it on top of the su with the rough side up. Put about ¾ c. rice mixture on ½ of the nori sheet, closest to you. Pack it firmly and evenly ~

When you roll it you won't want it to be too fat, so keep that in mind. Cut a ridge into the rice about ⅓ of the way up & lay in some thin strips of carrot & celery or cucumber, any combinations you like, but keep color in mind. Very gently, using su to begin, roll the nori away from you, tucking in the edge. Finish the roll with just your hands & use the su to round it out. Fill in the ends firmly with extra rice. With a very sharp knife slice the roll in ½" pieces, wiping the knife on a wet cloth between each cut. Serve with a little wasabi (very HOT) mixed with soy sauce to taste, & ginger on the side. ♥

To make Rice Cakes: Wet hands & salt well so rice won't stick to them. Put a Tbsp. of rice into your palm & make a firm little oval cake ⬭ about 1½" long. Peel the shrimp, leaving the tail on. Take a wooden pick & push it through the shrimp all the way up, making it very straight & flat. (Shrimp curl when boiled & you want them to cook flat & then lie flat on top of the rice cake.) Do all the shrimp in this manner and drop them, picks & all, into boiling water — when water comes back to boil, they are done. Cool them, then butterfly them, & remove vein. Lay them over rice cakes. Cut a ¼" strip of nori off a sheet & wrap it around the rice cake & shrimp just once. Cut off the extra & wet your finger & touch the edges of the nori so it will hold 🍣. Serve with ginger & the wasabi ~ soy sauce mixture. ♥ If a roll should ever split, you can fix it with a little bit of moistened nori. ♥ A simple, clean presentation is the hallmark of Japanese cooking, so be creative when serving sushi. ♥ Ideas for sushi rolls : a lovely combination would be thin slices of avocado, crab meat, & cucumber. Another would be lobster meat, radish, & celery. Try your own ideas. ♥

Rice cake with
radish sprouts ♥

# GUACAMOLE SHRIMP BITES

Makes about 60

Festive tasty treats. ♥

30 med. shrimp                          60 round tortilla chips
Guacamole (p.19)                        1 bunch cilantro (garnish)

Shell & devein the shrimp; drop them into boiling water.
Cook 2 min. (no more) ~ drain them & refresh them in cold water.
Make the guacamole & keep both shrimp & guacamole refrigerated
until ready to serve. When ready, spread each tortilla chip
with guacamole; cut the shrimp in half & place one shrimp-
half on each chip. Garnish each with one cilantro leaf & serve. ♥

# SMOKED BLUEFISH PÂTÉ

Makes 1½ cups

Creamy delicious ~ serve with crackers or fill celery stalks. ♥
   ⅓ lb. smoked bluefish            5 drops Tabasco sauce
   8 oz. cream cheese, softened     2 Tbsp. fresh dill, minced
   1 Tbsp. Worcestershire sauce     2 Tbsp. parsley, minced

"Crumble" the bluefish. Whip the cream cheese well & stir in
bluefish. Add all other ingredients & cream together. Refrigerate. ♥

# CREAM CHEESE & PESTO MOLD

### Makes about 6 cups

Buttery layers of cream cheese with pesto make a dramatic looking centerpiece at a party. ♥

1 lb. unsalted butter
2 8 oz. pkg. cream cheese
Pesto (recipe p. 81)

¼ c. pine nuts
1 Tbsp. butter
1 sprig fresh basil

You'll need a piece of cheesecloth, 18" square, double thickness, for this recipe & an 8 cup mold (a clean flowerpot will do fine!). Make the pesto. Cream the butter & cheese together until smooth & well blended. Wet the cheesecloth & wring it dry. Line the mold as smoothly as possible & drape excess over sides. You can have as many layers as you like, but you should start with the cheese & also end with it. I like alot of layers so I do 6 layers of cheese & 5 of pesto ~ it's best to divide the cheese and the pesto ahead of time so the layers will be even. After the mold is filled, fold the excess cheesecloth over the top & press down firmly. Refrigerate for 2 hours; then invert onto serving dish & gently remove cheesecloth. (can be covered with plastic wrap & refrigerated for up to 5 days.) Before serving, melt 1 Tbsp. butter in small skillet & cook the pine nuts over medium heat till lightly browned; drain on paper towels; cool. Arrange the nuts in a circle around the top of cheese; place a sprig of fresh basil in the center & serve. ♥ Crackers, bread & raw vegies are good accompaniments. ♥ I like to pile the cheese on fresh French bread & top it with a thick slice of radish. ♥

# STUFFED FRENCH BREAD

250°

I love how this looks at a Christmas party ~ a pretty, edible package. ♥ By changing the color of the ribbon, or by adding American flags, Valentines, or whatever, it would be darling at any celebration. ♥

2 8oz. pkg. cream cheese, softened    ½ c. minced green onion
2 cans chopped clams, drained    1 tsp. salt
2 Tbsp. lemon juice    1 Tbsp. Worcestershire sauce
½ c. chopped fresh parsley    ½ tsp. hot pepper sauce
2 round loaves of French bread

Mix ingredients ~ Cut off the top of one of the loaves of bread ~ hollow out the bottom part & fill it with the cream cheese mixture. Put the lid back on & wrap the loaf in foil. Bake at 250° for 3 hours. Cut the other loaf into dipping-sized pieces & serve alongside. For Christmas choose a wide plaid ribbon, set the lid off to the side a little, and hook the bow down with a straight pin ~ You'll want it to look like a Christmas present. ♥

# NASTURTIUMS

Serves Six

This is a spectacular summer appetizer ~ a plateful of big, beautiful (edible) orange flowers stuffed with a sweetened cream cheese mixture ~ Delicious! ♥ They grow them year-round in a wonderful solar greenhouse here on the island ~ you can grow them outside in the summer (they also deter pests & improve growth & flavor in your vegetable garden) or look for them in health food stores or gourmet food shops. ♥

3/4 c. cream cheese
4 Tbsp. sour cream
1 Tbsp. fresh lemon juice
3 tsp. honey

1 tsp. vanilla
1/3 c. chopped walnuts
1/4 c. chopped raisins
18 nasturtiums & leaves

Soften cream cheese. Blend all ingredients well (except for flowers). Form into tiny balls & chill 1/2 hour. Fit a ball into the center of each flower. Arrange on a plate covered with the large dark green nasturtium leaves. ♥ For extra prettiness, top each filled nasturtium with a fresh Violet 🌸 or a tiny Forget~me~not. 🌼 Other edible flowers include: Day Lily 🌸, Johnny~jump~up 🌸, & Gladiolus 🌸. ♥ Be sure no pesticides are used on the flowers, O.K.?

> "Things that haven't been done before,
> Those are the things to try;
> Columbus dreamed of an unknown shore
> At the rim of the far~flung sky."
> Edgar Guest ♥

# WONTON

Makes about 60

Serve these with Chinese Dumplings (p.13) & some hot sake for a nice change. ♥

1 lb. ground pork
1 egg, beaten
1 tsp. sesame oil
2 Tbsp. soy sauce
1 clove garlic, minced

4 Tbsp. green onion, minced
2 tsp. cornstarch
1 lb. wonton wrappers
peanut oil for frying
Sweet & Sour Sauce

Thoroughly combine pork, egg, sesame oil, soy sauce, garlic, green onion & cornstarch. Wonton wrappers dry out quickly so lay a damp cloth on your counter top & fold it in half. Put 1 tsp. of filling in the center of each wrapper; moisten edges with water & fold into triangle shape; put under damp cloth. Repeat until all filling is used. Heat about 4" oil in large pan over med. high heat. Fry wonton, a few at a time, until browned on both sides. Drain on paper towels & keep warm in a 200° oven till all are done. Serve hot. ♥ These can be frozen. To reheat, do not defrost; place on cookie sheet & bake 15 min. at 350°. ♥

## Sweet & Sour Sauce

2/3 c. brown sugar
2/3 c. rice wine vinegar
2/3 c. water
1/3 c. catsup

1½ Tbsp. soy sauce
2 tsp. Worcestershire sauce
2 tsp. ginger, minced
3 tsp. cornstarch

Combine sugar & vinegar in a saucepan & bring to boil. Reduce heat & simmer 5 min., stirring occasionally. Stir in all other ingredients & simmer 15 min. more. Serve hot with wonton. ♥

# FLOWERS & CHEESE

They're guaranteed to be the prettiest things at the party. ♥ The flowers keep their vibrant colors & the cheeses shimmer in the wine glaze. They make a beau— tiful house present. ♥

The last time I made these I used a petite Montrachet log, a wedge of Cheddar, a small wheel of Brie & a rectangular piece of jack. The different shapes & colors add texture but you definitely want to use cheese with an edible rind. For flowers (pesticide free) you can use nasturtiums, violets, roses, Johnny~jump-ups, lavender, chive flowers, honeysuckle or forget-me-nots— all edible. Sprigs & leaves of herbs are so delicate — use chives, rosemary, parsley, thyme & basil — just to name a few. Put the cold cheese on a wire rack in a shallow pan ~ arrange your flowers on top & then : Mix together 1 envelope plain gelatin & 2 cups good dry white wine in a saucepan & set aside for about 5 minutes. Cook over medium heat, stirring, till gelatin is dissolved & mixture is clear. Cool quickly by pouring into another bowl & setting it into a larger bowl of ice & water. Stir gently occasionally until mixture becomes syrupy. Remove flowers from cheese; spoon over your 1st coat of cooled gelatin; let it get a little tacky; lay on flowers the way you like them. Refrigerate 20 min., and spoon on another coat of gelatin. Again refrigerate & continue this way with a couple more coats ~ do sides & top & cover flowers completely. ♥ Gelatin can be reheated if it should become too thick. Cheeses can be made a day ahead & kept covered (invert a bowl over them) in your refrigerator till ready to serve. ♥ Simply beautiful!

"April in New England
is like first love."
♥ Gladys Taber ♥

# TRADITION

A lovely word that brings up childhood memories and feelings of security. With families going their own ways so much these days, some of the old traditions have been put aside and maybe even forgotten. But that doesn't mean you can't start new ones, better ones and even happier ones. The mother of one of my friends gives her a nightgown every Christmas 🎄. When she mentioned this she said it with kind of an embarrassed roll of the eyes ~ but it was obvious that the continuity of this tradition pleased her. She depends on that nightgown! 🎀 At our house we had the same menu every single Thanksgiving, and now to substitute or change anything for me would be doing major damage to Thanks~ giving! 🍂 Here are some other ideas for traditions, and I'm sure you can think of lots more:

- Have a guest book in your house ~ Ask for names and "Words of Wisdom, Quotes, etc." ~ a wonderful way to re~ member your friends and family on special occasions.
- Tie bells on the bread basket with a ribbon ~ passing the bread makes a nice happy Christmas sound.
- Chop down your own Christmas tree ~ make it a party with hot cider and popcorn.
- Easter egg hunt ~ Easter egg coloring party (p.117)
- Sunday dinners at four o'clock
- Sunday rides in the country
- Mom cooks your favorite on your birthday.
- Root beer floats made with homemade ice cream every 4th of July

# FOR YOUR GUESTS

♥ Clean fresh sheets and blankets on the bed.
♥ Flowers ~ one rose, a tiny bouquet of wildflowers...
♥ Make up a big plate of sandwiches, like roast beef with dilled Havarti cheese, sweet pickle, thinly sliced red onion and lettuce ~ good sandwiches! They'll be there all weekend when anyone is hungry & you can put them in a Styrofoam cooler with other goodies for the trip home.
♥ Have small picture books, magazines, quick reads.
♥ Plan things: a picnic, a concert, a hike in the woods.
♥ Put grapes and nuts in their room, and a container of fresh water with a glass.
♥ Have a fluffy covered hot water bottle.
♥ In the winter, summer herbs for good smells.
♥ Big Idea: My house is very tiny and I wanted a place for my guests to feel comfortable, so out in the backyard I built a little "shed" exactly the size of two king beds ~ ½ of it is bed, and the other half is chairs, a table, etc. It's whitewashed ~ dried flowers hang from the rafters ~ no electricity, but lots of candles & windows. Very cozy & romantic. ♥

# SOUPS

"It breathes reassurance, it offers consolation;
after a weary day it promotes sociability . . . .
There is nothing like a bowl of hot soup . . . . "
~ The Soup Book, Louis DeGouy ~

# CHICKEN STOCK

In comparison to rich homemade chicken stock, the canned stuff is like brown salted water ♥ It's very easy to make ~ and you'll love having the cooked chicken meat around for munching. ♥

1 lg. or 2 small chickens
hearts & gizzards from chicken
2 Tbsp. butter
1 Tbsp. oil
3 carrots, chopped
3 ribs of celery with leaves, chopped

1 lg. onion, chopped
2 bay leaves
1 bunch parsley
8 peppercorns
water to cover

Everything can be very roughly chopped & unpeeled as it will be cooked for hours & then strained out of the soup ~ all you want are the flavors & the vitamins. ♥ Melt the butter & oil in a deep soup pot ~ put in the chopped hearts & gizzards & fry over med. high heat. When well browned, add ½ c. water to pot & scrape brown bits off bottom ~ add all remaining ingredients. Leave chickens whole, or cut in half only. Fill pot with water just to cover. Bring to boil, then reduce heat to simmer & cook till chicken is done ~ about 1 hr. Remove chicken from pot; cool to touch. Remove all meat to your refrigerator & put the skin & bones back into the soup pot. Leave the pot simmering, with lid slightly askew, for about 3 hours or more ~ it doesn't really matter ~ but don't allow water level to get too low ~ add more when needed. When you're ready, strain the soup; discard the vegies & bones ~ put the broth in the refrigerator, uncovered, overnight. The fat will rise to the top, harden, & you can just scrape it right off. Beneath, you'll have a beautiful rich broth all ready to use for French Onion Soup (p. 34) & lots of others. ♥ If you want it for sauce or gravy, boil down till very strong; pour into ice cube trays; freeze; remove to plastic bags; use as needed. ♥

# CHICKEN BARLEY SOUP

*Makes 8~10 servings* ♥

Truly the magical elixir ~ the well-known cure for the common cold ♥.

Chicken Stock (p.32)
2 Tbsp. butter
1 lg. onion, chopped
2 c. barley, rinsed
3 carrots, sliced

3 stalks celery, sliced
1 c. parsley, minced
salt & pepper, to taste
chicken meat, chopped
Parmesan cheese (opt.)

Reheat the stock; taste for strength ~ if not strong enough, boil down till taste is correct. Melt butter in skillet; add onion & slow~cook till soft & golden. Rinse barley & pick over for rocks. When stock is boiling, add barley & simmer till the barley is almost cooked through & soft. Add slow~cooked onions, carrots, celery, & parsley. Cook until carrots are just tender. (Don't overcook the vegies!) Add salt & pepper & chopped chicken ~ Heat through and serve. Try a little Parmesan sprinkled on each serving. ♥ The amounts of vegetables & chicken can be altered, depending on how much broth you have. ♥ From a large chicken, I usually get about 8 cups of stock. ♥ If you'd rather have chicken ~potato soup, substitute diced potatoes for barley & add them at the same time as other vegetables. ♥ Sometimes, for a change of flavor, I add thyme to the soup. ♥ Experiment.!♥

# FRENCH ONION SOUP

Serves Six ♥

A hearty, classic soup. It's the long, slow cooking of the onions that brings out the mellow, rich flavor. ♥ Have it with a Caesar Salad (p. 52) for a nice cozy dinner ~ and baked bananas (p.162) for dessert. ♥

5 c. onions, thinly sliced
4 Tbsp. butter
1 clove garlic, minced
3 Tbsp. flour
8 c. rich chicken stock (p. 32)

1 tsp. thyme leaves
1 tsp. Dijon mustard
Freshly ground pepper
French bread croutons (below)
1 lb. Swiss or Gruyère cheese

Put the onions & butter in a large, heavy soup pan. Stir to coat with butter. Cover pan & cook very slowly for about 15 min., stirring once or twice. Uncover & cook for another half hour, stirring often until onions are golden brown ~ very slow cooking. Stir in garlic; cook 2~3 min. Add flour; stir & cook 2~3 min. more. Add stock, thyme, mustard & pepper (to taste). Bring to boil ~ lower heat & simmer 30~40 min. Put soup in oven-proof bowls. To each bowl add 2~3 French bread croutons ~ allow them to expand ~ they form the base for cheese to sit upon. Add about ½ c. grated cheese on top of each bowl. Bake in 425° oven for 30 min. till cheese is golden brown. ♥

## Croutons

Cut rounds of French bread about 3/4" thick. Place in 325° oven for 15 min. to dry. Brush both sides with olive oil ~ rub with cut garlic clove. Bake another 10~15 min. till lightly browned. ♥

♥ ♥ ♥

# BEAN SOUP

Serves Six

In late Fall, when the first chill comes, this is my first and favorite soup to make. It makes my house smell good as it slowly bubbles away the afternoon. This is the kind of soup that sticks to your ribs, and it's good for you too. ♥

1½ lbs. smoked ham hocks
1 lb. pkg. small white beans
3 sliced carrots
3 stalks celery, sliced

2 medium onions, chopped
2 bay leaves
salt and pepper to taste
water to cover

Put all ingredients in a soup pot. Bring to boil. Reduce heat and simmer partially covered for 3~4 hours. It will get very thick, so add water when you think it needs it. Somewhere down the line remove the ham hocks from the soup, and cool them. Cut the meat off the bones, discard the fat and return the meat and bones to the pot. When you're ready to serve, remove the bones and bay leaves & bring out some crusty bread and butter. ♥

Perhaps they are not stars, ☆ but rather openings in Heaven, where the love ☆ of our lost ones pours through & shines down upon us to let ☆ us know they are happy.
♥ Eskimo Legend

35

# TOMATO SOUP

Makes 4 cups

Make this in the summer when the tomatoes are the sweetest — it's clear, light, and elegant. Freeze some so you can enjoy the taste of summer all winter long. ♥

| | |
|---|---|
| 2½ lbs. fresh ripe tomatoes | 1 green pepper, chopped |
| 2 carrots, sliced | 3 whole cloves |
| 3 stalks celery, chopped | 2 Tbsp. lemon juice |
| 1 onion, chopped | salt and pepper |

Coarsely chop the tomatoes and put them in a soup pot with 1 cup water. Add carrots, celery, onion, green pepper, and cloves. Bring to a boil, reduce heat, and simmer for 20 minutes. Strain. Add lemon juice and salt and pepper to taste. Very few delicious calories. ♥

# KALE SOUP

Serves Eight

Full of good healthy things & somewhat of a tradition here on the island. ♥ Serve it with Best Biscuits, p.154. ♥

1 lb. kale, thoroughly washed
1 lb. linguica (or, sweet Italian sausage)
3 Tbsp. butter
2 Tbsp. olive oil
½ c. celery, chopped
1 c. onions, chopped
½ c. carrots, chopped
2 cloves garlic, minced

HEAT UP KITCHEN

4 med. potatoes, diced
8 c. Chicken Stock, p.32
2 c. canned beef broth
2 lbs. tomatoes, fresh or canned
1 19oz. can garbanzo beans
1 tsp. basil
1 tsp. thyme
salt, fresh pepper, to taste

Use tender part of kale only — leaves only, no stems. Chop into fairly small pieces — set aside. If using fresh tomatoes, peel, seed & chop them and set aside. Prick linguica with fork & drop into boiling water for 10 min., to get rid of the fat. Cut into ½" slices & quarter them. (If using Italian sausage, fry it; drain fat; reserve.) Melt the butter & oil in a large heavy soup pot; add celery, onions, carrots & garlic. Cook slowly till soft — add potatoes, chicken stock & beef broth. Bring to boil; reduce to simmer and cook, partially covered, for 15 min., till potatoes are cooked through. Stir in tomatoes & garbanzo beans. Simmer 15 min. more. Add kale, linguica (or sausage), basil, thyme and salt & pepper to taste. Simmer about 7 min. more — Serve. ♥

♥ ♥ ♥

" Chance is perhaps the pseudonym of God when
He did not want to sign." Anatole France ♥

# VICHYSSOISE

Serves Four

I have tasted many variations on this soup but this one has it all: creamy texture and delicate flavor. It can set the tone for an elegant dinner. ♥

1 ¼ lbs. leeks
1 small onion, chopped
¼ c. butter
1 ¾ lbs. potatoes, peeled and quartered
1 qt. chicken broth
1 Tbsp. fresh chives
1 tsp. dried chervil
1 tsp. salt
¼ tsp. white pepper
2 c. whole milk

Chop the white part only of leeks. Sauté the leeks and onion in melted butter in a 3-qt. saucepan over medium heat until onion is tender, about 10 min. Stir in potatoes and chicken broth. Heat to boiling — reduce heat — simmer uncovered for 45 min. Remove from heat — Cool slightly. Put half the potato mixture in blender & blend at high speed until puréed. Transfer to large bowl and repeat with remaining potato mixture. Stir in remaining ingredients, cover and chill well. ♥

# GAZPACHO

Serves Six

This is the freshest Gazpacho I've ever tasted ~ I think it's because it's not cooked. When I want to serve it as a main course, I add shrimp, sour cream, chives, & croutons to each serving. ♥

In your blender:
10 oz. cold tomato juice
½ med. cucumber, cut up
1 med. tomato, cut up
1 Tbsp. sugar
¼ c. red wine vinegar
¼ c. salad oil

To blended ingredients, add:
2½ c. tomato juice
1 med. tomato, chopped
½ med. cucumber, chopped
1 small onion, finely chopped
2 celery stalks, diced
2 green onions, green part only, chopped
½ zucchini, chopped
1 small green pepper, finely chopped

(Add or subtract any vegetables you like; make the pieces big enough to chew on, but not so big that they don't fit together on a spoon.) Serve very cold ~ make your own croutons (p. 52), add a big dollop of sour cream to each serving ~ and don't forget the shrimp. ♥

The past is a foreign country. They do things differently there.
♥ L. P. Hartley

39

# CIOPPINO

Serves 8~10

This special soup should be served in very wide~mouthed, shallow bowls ~ it is almost like a stew. It's also lots of fun to eat and has a thin delicious broth. ♥

3/4 c. butter
2 medium onions, chopped
2 garlic cloves, minced
1 large bunch fresh parsley, finely chopped
2 cans (1 lb. 12 oz.) whole tomatoes
2 cans (14 oz.) chicken broth
2 bay leaves
1 Tbsp. basil
½ tsp. each : thyme and oregano
1 c. water
1½ c. dry white wine
1½ lbs. extra large shrimp
1½ lbs. scallops (small "Bay" are sweetest)
1½ dozen fresh small clams
1½ dozen fresh mussels
1½ c. crabmeat chunks
Any other firm whitefish you'd like

Melt butter in a large kettle, add onions, garlic and parsley ~ cook slowly until onion is soft. Add tomatoes (breaking into chunks) with the liquid, broth, bay leaves, basil, thyme, oregano, water and wine. Cover and simmer 30 min. Add all fish, and bring to a boil. Cover and simmer 5~7 min., till the clams are open. Serve hot with a Spinach Salad (p.53) and garlic bread (p.66). ♥

40

# Coconut, Ginger, & Lime Soup

Serves 4

This make-ahead, ice-cold soup, at the end of a hot day, is just what the doctor ordered. Have it w/ hot crusty French bread & a creamy chevre. 

1 tbsp. toasted sesame oil
2 tbsp. minced ginger
4 c. chicken stock
1~13.5 oz. can coconut milk
½ lb. shitake mushrooms, sliced
1 lg. carrot, shredded
1 tbsp. chili puree w/garlic
½ tsp. salt

zest of one lime
2 tbsp. lime juice
opt. 1 lb. med. shrimp, cleaned, cut into bite-sized pieces
opt. 6 oz. med. egg noodles, cooked & rinsed
⅓ c. each, chopped basil, cilantro & green onions, green part only

Heat oil in lg. saucepan, add ginger, sizzle for a minute. Pour in chicken stock, simmer 10 min. Add coconut milk, mushrooms, carrot, chili puree, & salt. Simmer 10 min. Stir in lime zest & juice. If you're having shrimp, add them & simmer 2-3 min. until just done; remove from heat (don't overcook shrimp). Add cooked noodles if you choose. Stir in herbs (keep a sprinkling for garnish). Cool soup; pour into serving dish & chill. Before serving, stir well & garnish.

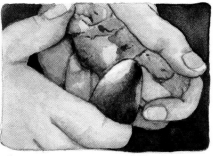

PEELING GINGER w/ A SPOON

# BUTTERNUT BISQUE

Serves Six

Rich orange color ~ thickened with potato rather than cream ~ very nutritious & low-calorie. ♥

2-2½ lb. Butternut squash
2 Tbsp. butter
2 carrots, sliced
1 onion, chopped
1 stalk celery, chopped

2 potatoes, peeled & cubed
5-6 c. chicken stock (canned is OK)
1½ tsp. curry powder
pinch each: nutmeg & ginger
sour cream for garnish (opt.)

My market peels & seeds their squash, which is very handy as it must be done for this soup. Cube it & set aside. Melt the butter in a lg. soup pot; add the carrots, onion & celery; sauté until soft. Stir the squash & potatoes into the vegetables. Add the stock; bring to boil, reduce heat & simmer, partially covered for 40 min. Add curry, nutmeg & ginger. Purée the soup in batches in a blender. Return to saucepan; add more stock if necessary to thin; salt & pepper to taste. Serve hot with a dollop of sour cream if you like. ♥

"By December the valley people are really dug in for winter. Wood is piled high in sheds, cabbages and pots are binned in the cellars, and squash and apples are stored." ♥

Gladys Taber ♥

# CREAM OF CAULIFLOWER

### Serves Four

Good hot or cold — very quick to make. ♥ Purée in batches — be sure not to fill the blender too full with the hot liquid.

2 c. leeks, chopped
2 Tbsp. butter
2 Tbsp. oil
1 large head cauliflower (4c.)

4 c. chicken broth
1 c. milk
½ tsp. white pepper
2 Tbsp. snipped chives

Sauté leeks in butter & oil till soft & golden. Add cauliflower & chicken broth; bring to boil; reduce to simmer & cook until cauliflower is soft. Purée mixture in blender or food processor. Return to pan; add milk & pepper; reheat slowly (don't boil). Before serving, sprinkle with snipped chives. ♥

"The night shall be filled with music
And the cares that infest the day
Shall fold their tents like the Arabs,
And as silently steal away."
♥ Henry Wadsworth Longfellow

# FISH CHOWDER

### Serves Eight

Serve with a big basket of Cornmeal Muffins (p.156). ♥

| | |
|---|---|
| 2½~3 lb. whole cod fish | 3 lg. potatoes, diced |
| 2 pt. oysters, shucked | 2 med. onions, chopped |
| 2 pt. clams, shucked | 1 potato, grated |
| 2 ribs celery, chopped | 1 pt. half & half |
| 1 small onion, chopped | ½ c. heavy cream |
| ¼ c. parsley, chopped | 3 Tbsp. butter |
| 6 thick slices bacon | salt & pepper, to taste |

Select a whole fish; ask the fish man to clean & filet it & chop the carcass to fit into soup pot. Reserve filets; put the carcass, the liquid from the oysters and clams, the celery, onion & parsley into a pot. Barely cover with water. Bring to boil & simmer, uncovered, until liquid boils down to about 2 cups. Meanwhile, cook the bacon crisp~remove from fat; reserve. Cook the potatoes in the bacon fat till tender; add onions, cook through & remove from heat. Strain the fish broth; return broth to pot & add grated potato. Simmer for 10 min; add potato onion mixture, oysters, clams & cod fish (cut into 1½" pieces). Cook gently 5 min. Stir in half & half, cream, butter, crumbled bacon, & salt & pepper to taste. (Thin with milk if necessary.) Heat through, but don't boil  Remove from heat; allow the soup to sit 1 hr. Reheat & serve. ♥

"I must go down to the seas again, to the lonely sea and the sky,
And all I ask is a tall ship and a star to steer her by ..." J.Masefield

# ZUCCHINI SOUP

Serves Four

This tasty light soup resolves the problem of what to do with all those giant zucchinis your "friends" leave on your porch!

4 c. sliced zucchini
1 med. onion, chopped
3 Tbsp. butter
1 c. water
1 10 oz. can cream of chicken soup
1 c. milk
1 c. half & half
1 tsp. dried basil
salt and pepper

Sauté onion in butter several minutes. Add zucchini and water ~ Simmer 30 min. Remove from heat; cool slightly. Blend in blender at high speed until puréed. Return to saucepan. Add the rest of the ingredients and heat to simmering. Serve. ♥

"Hitch your wagon to a star."
Emerson ♥

Girl   Bill   Man

'Tis merry, merry in the spring,
And merry in the summer time,
And merry when the great winds sing
Through autumn's woodlands brown—
And in the winter, wild and cold,
'Tis merry, merry too. ♥

William Howitt

# SALAD DRESSINGS

## Cheese and Herb

Makes 1¼ cups

1 c. mayonnaise
2 Tbsp. fresh lemon juice
⅓ c. grated Parmesan cheese

½ c. minced parsley
1 tsp. dried tarragon
1 clove minced garlic (opt.)

Mix well, cover & refrigerate. ♥

## Balsamic Vinaigrette

¼ c. balsamic vinegar
2 anchovies, mashed
1 Tbsp. Dijon mustard
1 clove garlic, crushed

1 Tbsp. parsley, minced
1 Tbsp. fresh rosemary leaves
½ c. olive oil

Whisk together vinegar, anchovies, & mustard; add garlic,
parsley & rosemary. In a thin stream, whisk in olive oil. ♥

## Cream

Makes ½ cup

⅓ c. heavy cream
3 tsp. fresh lemon juice
½ tsp. white pepper

¼ tsp. salt
1 Tbsp. olive oil
1 Tbsp. peanut oil

Beat first four ingredients with whisk till foamy
and creamy. Beat in oil slowly. Especially good on
tender greens such as Boston or Bibb lettuce. ♥

## Poppy Seed

Makes 1½ cups

1 egg yolk
1 tsp. Dijon mustard
3 Tbsp. honey
¼ c. lemon juice

1 tsp. paprika
Fresh pepper to taste
1 c. oil
1½ Tbsp. poppy seeds

Put all ingredients except oil & poppy seeds into food processor & blend well. Slowly add oil until thickened. Stir
in poppy seeds; cover & refrigerate. ♥

## Cottage Cheese

Makes 1½ cups

1 c. cottage cheese
¼ c. buttermilk
1 tsp. dill weed
1 Tbsp. parsley, minced

½ tsp. celery seed
Fresh pepper to taste
½ green pepper, minced
2 Tbsp. bleu cheese

Put the cottage cheese & buttermilk into blender ~ Blend well;
pour into container Add all other ingredients & mix well.
Cover & refrigerate. ♥

## Diet

Makes 2½ cups

¼ c. apple juice
¼ c. fresh lemon juice
1 c. vegetable juice
⅓ c. green onion, minced

1 clove garlic, minced
⅓ c. celery, chopped
¼ c. parsley, minced
fresh pepper to taste

Blend all in blender; cover & refrigerate. ♥

# MAYONNAISE

## Makes 2 cups

With a food processor, it takes about 5 minutes to make your own mayonnaise and you won't believe the difference. ♥ Use it as is. For a special chicken salad, add a little curry & chutney to taste. ♥

1 whole egg
2 egg yolks
3 Tbsp. fresh lemon juice
1 Tbsp. Dijon mustard

Freshly ground pepper & salt, to taste
1 c. olive oil
1 c. vegetable oil

Put the egg, yolks, lemon juice, mustard, pepper & salt into food processor and blend 1 minute. Blend the olive & vegetable oils together; then, with machine running, pour in the oil in a very slow, steady stream. That's it! Feel free to add any herbs you like to make flavored mayonnaise. ♥

# TARTAR SAUCE

## Makes 1 cup

Best made with homemade mayonnaise ~ delicious with fish. ♥ Yummy with french fries. ♥

1 c. mayonnaise
1 Tbsp. capers
1 Tbsp. minced parsley

2 tsp. minced green onion
2 tsp. minced sweet pickle
1½ Tbsp. cider vinegar

Blend all ingredients & refrigerate. ♥

# CHICKEN SALAD

Serves Six

I bake up chickens all the time just so I always have "leftovers". ♡ This healthy salad is one reason why. ♡

2 c. cooked cubed chicken
2 ribs celery, chopped
1 green apple, cored & chopped
½ c. chopped walnuts

½ c. cubed Cheddar cheese
3 minced green onions
⅓ c. mayonnaise mixed with juice from ½ lemon

Mix all ingredients and serve on a bed of crisp lettuce leaves, torn in bite-sized pieces. ♡

# EDIBLE SALAD BOWLS

These make adorable little salad bowls. You'll need a pkg. of egg roll skins (about 7" x 7") and 3 inches of hot oil (at about 375°). Lay egg roll skin flat on surface of oil ~ submerge, pressing with ladle to form bowls. When brown & crisp, drain upside-down on paper towels. Cool; fill with salad and serve. ♥

# CAESAR SALAD

Serves Six

Lots of people turn their noses up to anchovies, so either mash them up very well, or use a food processor. They'll never know, and the anchovies add a delicious tang to the salad. ♥

1 lg. head romaine lettuce
½ c. olive oil
¼ c. fresh lemon juice
1 tbsp. Dijon mustard
1 2oz. can anchovies

1 lg. egg
½ tsp. freshly ground
    pepper
⅓ c. grated Parmesan
2 c. homemade croutons

Wash lettuce early in the day so it has time to dry completely. Put the oil, lemon juice, mustard, anchovies, and egg into food processor and process for just a few seconds. Tear romaine into bite-sized pieces and put in salad bowl. Pour mixture over lettuce, sprinkle on pepper, Parmesan, and croutons. Toss the salad lightly and serve. ♥

# HOMEMADE CROUTONS

Melt 2 parts butter to 1 part olive oil in a large skillet over medium high heat. Add 1 minced garlic clove. Cut french bread into ½" cubes. Don't overcrowd the skillet. Toss often to avoid burning. Toast well on all sides. ♥ These keep well in an airtight container. Delicious for salads and soups. ♥

# SPINACH SALAD

Serves Six

I don't like bacon grease on my spinach salad! So I made up this slightly sweet dressing that seems to compliment the spinach just right. ♥ For extra crunch & prettiness, scatter pomegranate seeds over the salad. ♥

1 bunch spinach
½ c. cider vinegar
⅓ c. salad oil
¼ c. brown sugar

Freshly ground pepper &
Salt, to taste
4 hard-boiled egg whites
6 slices bacon, fried

Wash spinach very thoroughly and dry. Hard-boil eggs; fry the bacon till crispy, cool. Chop white parts of eggs only and reserve. (Save yolks for an egg salad.) In a shaker jar, mix vinegar, oil, brown sugar, salt & pepper. Shake well. Pour over spinach torn in bite-sized pieces. Toss lightly. Sprinkle on eggwhites and crumbled bacon. Serve. ♥

"'It's broccoli, dear.'
'I say it's spinach, and
I say the hell with it.'"
E.B. White ♥

# SHRIMP SALAD

A refreshing combination of flavors ~ very bright. ♥
    Large cooked shrimp, chopped
    Avocado (thick & bumpy skinned)
    Fresh pink grapefruit sections
    Mayonnaise
    Orange juice
Put an equal amount of chopped shrimp, cubed avocado & pink grapefruit sections into a bowl. Dress with a little mayonnaise sweetened & thinned with orange juice. Serve chilled. ♥

# CRAB SALAD

You can serve this on toasted English muffins, on top of a chilled avocado half or on a bed of crisp lettuce. ♥
    2 c. fresh or frozen crab meat
    1/3. c mayonnaise
    2 Tbsp. fresh lemon juice
    3 green onions, minced
    2 stalks celery, finely chopped
    2 tsp. celery seed
Chop the crab meat & combine with all other ingredients. Chill before serving. ♥

# CEVICHE

Serves Four as Salad

Fifteen years ago I went to Mexico City quite often, where I discovered Ceviche. I loved it ~ in fact, I would get off the plane and go directly to the restaurant in the airport for my Ceviche "fix" ~ I can still eat it by the gallon! The secret is to use fish that is practically still alive ~ it has to be fresh. The juice from the limes "cooks" the fish, and along with the fresh vegetables, you can't find a dish much healthier or better tasting. ♥

1 lb. fresh bay scallops
juice from 8 limes
2 tomatoes, finely chopped
5 green onions with tops, minced
2 ribs of celery, thinly sliced

½ green pepper, minced
½ c. parsley, minced
freshly ground pepper
1½ Tbsp. finest olive oil
⅛ c. fresh cilantro, minced (opt)

Rinse the scallops and put them in a bowl with lime juice to cover. Chill all day or overnight until the scallops are opaque. After that, pour off about half of the juice and add the remaining ingredients. Mix well and serve chilled. ♥ Feel free to experiment with this ~ if you like more or less of some vegetables, add or subtract. Cilantro is a wonderful herb used in many Mexican dishes ~ it looks like parsley ~ and I know it's unavailable in some places. So, it's optional, but it does add the authentic flavor. Also, if you can't get bay scallops, you can use a pound of any very fresh boned white fish, such as halibut, red snapper, flounder, or swordfish. ♥ Make up a bowl of this and keep it around for summer munching. ♥

NOTE FROM THE FUTURE: Cilantro is everywhere. Yay!

# TABBOULI

Serves Six

Delicious, nutritious and highly addictive!
Serve it on a bed of crisp lettuce. ♥

1 c. bulgar wheat
5 green onions, minced
2 tomatoes, diced
½ c. parsley, minced
3 Tbsp. fresh mint, minced
1 lg. carrot, grated
5 Tbsp. olive oil
⅓ c. fresh lemon juice
Freshly ground pepper, to taste

Put the bulgar in a bowl with cold water to cover. Let
stand for 1 hour to soften. Drain well & squeeze
dry in a towel. Toss in a bowl with all
other ingredients. Chill well to blend
flavors. ♥

# STUFFED ARTICHOKES
### Serves Six

A hearty first course, or a delicious light lunch served with creamy, crispy Fried Brie (p. 14). ♥

6 large artichokes
6 extra-large shrimp, peeled & cleaned
1 c. crab meat
1 large tomato, diced
3/4 c. mayonnaise
curry powder, to taste
squeeze of lemon; paprika for color

Wash & trim artichokes; boil in salted water till stem is tender when pierced with fork. Cool and refrigerate. Drop shrimp into boiling water ~ when it comes back to boil, simmer for 1 min.; drain & refresh in cold water. Chill. When ready to serve, remove artichokes from the refrigerator, lightly spread leaves apart with your fingers & pull out the "choke," the tiny center leaves, making a cavity for filling. Scrape the bottom of cavity with spoon to remove "feathers." Mix mayonnaise with curry powder to taste. Chop shrimp & combine with crab meat, tomato, and just enough curried mayonnaise to bind. Fill the arti-chokes, squeeze lemon juice over all & sprinkle lightly with paprika. Serve with remaining mayonnaise for dipping. ♥

Memories mean more to me than dresses.
♥ Anne Frank

# POTATO SALAD

Serves Eight

The fans go crazy for this delicious and different potato salad. Have it for a picnic or a barbecue. ♥

2 lbs. red potatoes, scrubbed & halved
½ lb. bacon, chopped
½ c. shallots, finely chopped
¼ c. olive oil
½ c. red wine vinegar
1 c. parsley, finely chopped
½ c. red onion, chopped
½ c. celery, chopped
salt & freshly ground pepper

Boil potatoes till fork~tender, drain them, cut them into bite-sized pieces, and put them in a large bowl. Fry the bacon crisp and reserve. Pour out all but about 3 Tbsp. of the bacon fat & sauté the shallots in the fat very slowly, till soft. Pour the shallots & the bacon fat over the hot potatoes; add the oil, vinegar, parsley, onion, celery, and crumbled bacon. Toss very gently, but thoroughly. Salt & pepper to taste. Serve at room temperature. Cover & refrigerate leftovers. ♥

"Good Americans, when they die, go to Paris."
Thomas Appleton ♥

# PASTA SALAD

### Serves Fifteen (or more)

A great big colorful salad that's perfect for large crowds ~ barbecues & picnics ⚑. Also, good just to have around to appease the munchies. ♥

1 lb. corkscrew pasta      2 sweet red peppers, chopped
½ lb. tortellini with cheese      1 green pepper, chopped
½ c. plus 1 tbsp. olive oil      1 6 oz. can pitted black olives
6 cloves garlic, minced      4 tomatoes, chopped
1 bunch broccoli, in small flowerettes      1 c. Parmesan cheese, grated
2 med. zucchini, sliced & quartered      ½ c. Romano cheese, grated
1½ c. snow peas (or 2 pkg. frozen)      Freshly ground pepper

Cook the pasta according to package instructions. Drain & put into a large bowl. Pour oil into saucepan; add garlic & cook slowly till garlic is light brown. Set aside to cool. Lightly blanch broccoli, zucchini, and snow peas ~ refresh in cold water & set aside. Toss the pasta with garlic oil ~ add rest of ingredients & toss very gently. Serve. ♥ Two things of importance: don't let garlic get dark-colored while cooking in oil AND don't overcook blanched vegies ~ they should be firm in shape, but tender to the bite. ♥ Best served at room temperature. ♥ "America! America!

JULY 4ᵀᴴ PICNIC      God shed His grace on thee." ♥ K. Bates

61

# RAINBOW JELL-O

~~I'm not a big Jell-O fan, but~~ I love Jell-O & this one is so gorgeous and so delicious — you'll have to try it for a holiday dinner. The kids love it and the cold, smooth texture is a nice contrast in a heavy holiday meal. ♥

1 6 oz. pkg. orange Jell-O
1 6 oz. pkg. lemon Jell-O
1 6 oz. pkg. lime Jell-O
1 6 oz. pkg. cherry Jell-O
4 c. (2 pints) sour cream

Dissolve the orange Jell-O in 2 c. boiling water. To ½ c. of the liquefied Jell-O, add 1 c. sour cream and stir well. Pour sour cream/Jell-O mixture into a 9×13 glass baking dish and reserve remaining 1½ c. orange Jell-O. Put the baking dish on a level shelf of your refrigerator and chill until set. When firm, pour reserved orange Jell-O over creamy layer; chill until firm. Repeat with remaining colors of Jell-O— each with a creamy layer and a clear layer. ♥

"Glory be to God for dappled things."
♥ Gerard M. Hopkins ♥

# GREEN BEAN SALAD
### Serves Four

One more good reason to have a garden! Fresh green beans with garlic, red pepper & dill — very pretty, very good. ♥

1 lb. fresh green beans
3 Tbsp. olive oil
3 Tbsp. fresh lemon juice
2 cloves garlic, minced
1 shallot, minced

2 Tbsp. red pepper, minced
1 Tbsp. dill, minced
⅛ tsp. dry mustard
¼ tsp. salt
⅛ tsp. freshly ground pepper

Wash & trim ends of green beans but leave them whole. Cook the beans in boiling water for about 5 min. (they should still be crisp). Refresh immediately in cold water; set aside. Combine all remaining ingredients & mix well. Pour over beans & refrigerate 1 hour before serving. Serve cool, but not cold. ♥

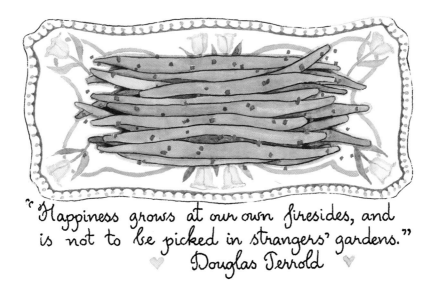

"Happiness grows at our own firesides, and is not to be picked in strangers' gardens."
Douglas Jerrold ♥

# FRUIT COMPOTE

350° Serves Six

Absolutely delicious. ♥ Use unsweetened fruit for this.
It would be great with ham, Cornish Game Hens (p.108),
or Veal Birds (p.92). Pour over heavy cream and you
can also serve it for dessert. ♥

| | |
|---|---|
| 1 can pineapple slices | ½ c. apricot juice |
| 1 can peach halves | 4 Tbsp. butter, melted |
| 1 can apricots | ½ c. brown sugar |
| 1 can pear halves | ½ c. coarsely chopped walnuts |

Preheat oven to 350°. Drain fruit well ~ reserve apricot
juice. Arrange dry fruit in baking dish. Cover with
mixture of apricot juice (½ c.), melted butter & brown
sugar. Sprinkle on walnuts; bake for 30 minutes
till bubbly. Serve hot. ♥

"I do not count the hours I spend
In wandering by the sea;
The forest is my loyal friend,
Like God it useth me."
Ralph W. Emerson

# Bean Salad
Serves Fifteen or more

This is a delicious munchable salad. ❤ If you're avoiding animal protein you can add rice to this dish making a complete vegetable protein. ❤

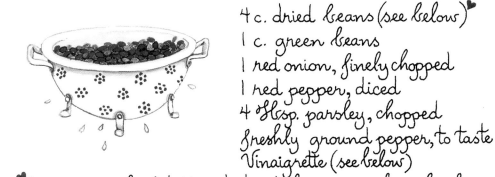

4 c. dried beans (see below)❤
1 c. green beans
1 red onion, finely chopped
1 red pepper, diced
4 Tbsp. parsley, chopped
freshly ground pepper, to taste
Vinaigrette (see below)

❤Use 1 cup each of different dried beans ~ make color be part of the criterion ~ choose from pinto beans, kidney beans, white beans, lentils, lima beans or garbanzo beans. Wash & pick over beans for rocks. Cook each kind of bean (including green beans) separately in boiling water till tender but <u>NOT</u> <u>MUSHY</u>. Put them all in a large bowl; add onion, red pepper, parsley & pepper. Pour over Vinaigrette & mix gently. Refrigerate to allow flavors to "marry". Serve. ❤

## Vinaigrette
½ c. olive oil                    4 cloves garlic, minced
¾ c. red wine vinegar   2 tsp. oregano
1 tsp. dry mustard        salt & pepper (opt.)
Whisk all ingredients together; pour over Bean Salad. ❤

# Coleslaw

### Serves Eight

Fresh, healthy, crunchy, & delicious ~ for an elegant lunch, top each serving with lobster meat, garnish with radish sprouts, & pass the best garlic bread in the world. ♥

- 1 head white cabbage, as thinly sliced as humanly possible
- 2 crisp, sweet apples (for juiciest best, try "Honeycrisp") cut into matchsticks
- 3/4 c. golden raisins
- 1/2 c. sliced almonds
- salt & freshly ground pepper

Add more or less of these ingredients depending on size of cabbage & your taste. Mix well with dressing & serve. ♥

## Dressing

1 c. mayonnaise whisked together with juice of three limes to consistency a little thinner than heavy cream.

# My Dad's Garlic Bread

The Stewart Family Garlic Bread is so tried & so true there are no words for it ~ delicious with everything. ♥

You need: 1 lg. loaf sourdough bread, sliced
         1 stick butter & 4 cloves garlic, thinly sliced

Melt butter together with garlic till it begins to bubble. Brush butter and slices of garlic onto bread. Broil until toasty brown. Watch closely, it burns easily. Yum!

# EGGPLANT SALAD
## with Yogurt Dressing

Serves Four

Fresh & tangy & just a little bit different ♥.

Yogurt Dressing (see below)
1 med. eggplant
salt
olive oil

1 bunch watercress
1 bunch red leaf lettuce
minced chives for garnish

Make the Yogurt Dressing & refrigerate. Peel & thinly slice eggplant.  Sprinkle it with salt & let stand ½ hour (removes bitterness). Rinse in cool water & pat dry.  Sauté in hot oil until crisp; drain on paper towels. Put watercress & lettuce leaves (any greens will do, but the more interesting, the better) on individual salad dishes; arrange eggplant on top & spoon over Yogurt Dressing. Sprinkle on chives & serve. ♥

## Yogurt Dressing

1 c. plain yogurt
2 tbsp. olive oil
1 tsp. garlic powder
½ tsp. basil
juice of 1 lemon

Mix all ingredients together & beat well. Cover & refrigerate. ♥

# MAKE YOUR OWN
## PLACE CARDS

Put this page onto a copier (or scan it) & print it out on card stock ~ cut out as many as you need. Fold back on dotted line & they will sit up like little soldiers on your table.

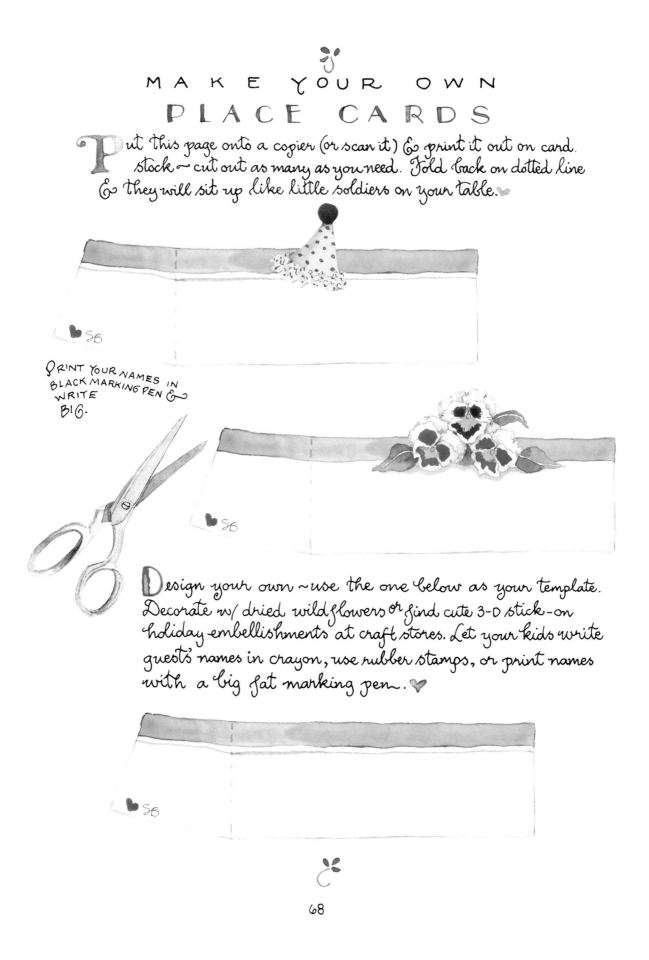

PRINT YOUR NAMES IN BLACK MARKING PEN & WRITE BIG.

Design your own ~ use the one below as your template. Decorate w/ dried wildflowers or find cute 3-D stick-on holiday embellishments at craft stores. Let your kids write guests' names in crayon, use rubber stamps, or print names with a big fat marking pen.

# VEGETABLES

"Eat your vegetables!"
~Mom~

# KITCHEN GARDENS

When most of us think of a garden we imagine the rows and rows of different vegetables, each variety demanding its own special treatment. We should worry about the soil needs, possible use of insecticides, mulches, and the necessity for the right amount of space. Then comes V-Day — drop everything! The garden is UP! Time for picking, digging, canning, drying and replanting. I don't know about you, but this is not my idea of a fun summer. ♥ But there is another type of garden that I do like to grow, which gives me the lovely satisfaction of having fresh food to serve without the intense amount of work involved in a large garden. I call it my "Kitchen Garden". ♥

I found a small plot of ground right outside my kitchen door, a perfect place for running out to pick a few herbs, some leaves of lettuce, or a tomato or two. I planted my favorite herbs — parsley, basil, camomile, dill, tarragon, mint, thyme and rosemary — then, two tomato plants, six heads of leaf lettuce (you don't pick the whole thing at once, just a leaf at a time as needed), radishes, some garlic and chives and flowers to fill in. I did take the time to prepare the soil, but since it was such a small area, it didn't take long at all and was well worth the trouble. After that I went right to the nursery and bought "starts," small plants all ready for planting — it took ½ hour to plant everything. ♥ Oh! One more thing, if you live where winters are mild, do include a dwarf lemon tree in your Kitchen Garden ~ Imagine! Fresh lemons right outside your kitchen door! Anyway ~ the only "insecticide" I used was the interspersing of marigolds among the vegetables and herbs to deter certain types of bugs. The garlic and chives also help to control pests. After that, all I had to do was water ~ and for my trouble I had perfectly fresh salads every day, and lovely herbs to use in everything imaginable, including camomile flowers to boil for steam facials, and fresh flowers for my little vases.

So, if you only have a little space, or you've never gardened before, I suggest you try a Kitchen Garden of your own. ♥ It's fun, and easy and very rewarding. ♥

"We are rarely ill, and if we are, we go off somewhere and eat grass until we feel better." ♥
                                        Paul Gallico

# STUFFED ZUCCHINI

350° Serves Six

This has so many healthy ingredients and tastes so good that sometimes I make it a meal all by itself ~ and go to bed skinny!

3 medium zucchini
1 green pepper, chopped
2 tomatoes, chopped
1 onion, finely chopped
1 clove garlic, minced
½ c. parsley, minced

1 tsp. oregano
juice of ½ lemon
salt & pepper
1½ c. vegetable juice
2 c. grated jack cheese
3 slices sourdough toast

Preheat oven to 350°. Cut the zucchini in half length~wise. Hollow out the zucchini by scooping out the pulp, reserving the shells. Chop the pulp & put it in a large skillet along with green pepper, tomatoes, onion, garlic, parsley, oregano, lemon juice, salt and pepper to taste, and ¾ c. of the vegetable juice. Cook slowly till vegetables are soft. Pile the mixture into the zucchini shells. Distribute the cheese equally over the tops. Cube the toast & put the pieces on top of the stuffing. Put the zucchini in a baking pan & pour the remaining ¾ c. vegetable juice around them. Bake 30 minutes. Spoon hot juice over.

# GLAZED CARROTS

## Serves Six

Bright orange color & a shimmer of glaze ~ They look best cut on the diagonal. ♥ Complimentary to almost any dinner. ♥

1½ lb. carrots, cut into 2" pieces
2 Tbsp. butter
½ c. brown sugar
2 c. orange juice, fresh is best ♥
⅛ tsp. orange zest
1¼ Tbsp. cornstarch
pinch of ginger

Peel the carrots & steam them just to tender crisp; set aside. In saucepan combine butter, sugar, orange juice & orange zest. Heat mixture until it begins to bubble ~ whisk in cornstarch & cook over medium heat until thickened. Add ginger & carrots to saucepan ~ stir gently ~ pour into serving dish. ♥

"One honest John Tompkins, a hedger and ditcher,
Although he was poor, did not want to be richer;
For all such vain wishes in him were prevented
By a fortunate habit of being contented." ♥
♥ Jane Taylor

# SPRING MEDLEY

Serves Six

I _love_ this dish ~ it's quick, easy, elegant & delicious ~ my four favorite things in cooking!

½ c. butter
3 bunches of radishes, sliced
4 bunches of watercress
squeeze of lemon juice
freshly ground pepper
Parmesan cheese (opt.)

Melt half the butter in a large skillet; sauté the radishes until almost tender (but still crisp), 4~5 min. Remove to serving dish. Remove the large tough stems from the watercress & sauté it in the remaining butter just till wilted ~ 2 to 3 min. Put the radishes back into the skillet with the watercress; add freshly ground pepper & a squeeze of lemon juice. Heat through, pour into serving dish & add a sprinkle of Parmesan cheese if you like. ♥ I have also made this with spinach when I couldn't get watercress & it was very good. ♥

Garden tip: plant nasturtiums amongst radishes ~ they deter pests & radishes love them. ♥

# HOT CHERRY TOMATOES

Serves Four

A colorful side dish ~ easy & quick to make ~ but still an elegant accompaniment for almost any main course. ♥

2 Tbsp. butter
1 Tbsp. olive oil
1 clove garlic, minced
1 basket med. cherry tomatoes
2 Tbsp. fresh basil, minced ~ Or,
2 Tbsp. fresh parsley, minced

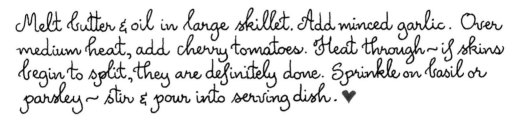

Melt butter & oil in large skillet. Add minced garlic. Over medium heat, add cherry tomatoes. Heat through ~ if skins begin to split, they are definitely done. Sprinkle on basil or parsley ~ stir & pour into serving dish. ♥

# ASPARAGUS ON TOAST

A delicious & different way to serve asparagus. ♥

Lay spears of tender cooked asparagus on a toasted slice of bread. Sprinkle over about 1 Tbsp. of the water asparagus was cooked in. Pour melted butter over all & serve. ♥

# ONION PUDDING

350° Serves Four

Cheesy, filled with caramelized onions, delicious with roast chicken (p. 91), perfect with my mom's Spareribs & Juice (p. 105).

3 c. water
½ c. rice
1 tsp. salt
¼ c. butter
4 lg. yellow onions
  chopped, ½" pieces

A good, full cup of
  grated Swiss cheese
½ c. chopped walnuts
2/3 c. milk or half-n-half
¼ c. shredded Parmesan
  cheese

Preheat oven to 350°. Bring water to boil; stir in rice & salt; cook 5 min.; rinse, drain, & put rice in a large bowl. Melt butter in large skillet. Cook onions, stirring often over high heat until they brown. Put onions in bowl with rice. Stir in Swiss cheese, walnuts, salt & pepper to taste, and milk. Pour into baking dish, sprinkle with Parmesan. Bake 1 hour. ♥

Oh, I adore to cook. It makes me feel
so mindless in a worthwhile way.
♥ Truman Capote

# PURÉED VEGETABLES

Sometimes you need a dish with a special texture to round out your menu. Either of these can fill the bill. They both have bright color, smooth texture & delicious flavor. ♥

## Carrot Purée

Serves Four

5 medium carrots, sliced
2 Tbsp. butter, melted
2 Tbsp. rum

5-6 Tbsp. heavy cream
salt & pepper, to taste

Preheat oven to 350°. Wash and slice the carrots. Cook them in boiling water till tender; set aside. Melt butter in a small saucepan, stir in rum & 5 Tbsp. cream ~ heat till steaming, but don't boil. Put the carrots in a food processor, add butter sauce & whirl to smooth consistancy. Add additional Tbsp. of cream if you think it needs it. Stir in salt & pepper; remove to heat proof dish & reheat in oven for 10~15 min. Serve. ♥

## Puréed Peas

Serves Four

1 10 oz. pkg. frozen peas
2 slices bacon, chopped
⅓ c. water

2 Tbsp. butter
5 Tbsp. heavy cream
salt & pepper, to taste

Put the peas & bacon in a small saucepan with ⅓ c. water. Cover & cook till peas are tender; drain. Put the peas (with the bacon) in the food processor; add the butter & cream & whirl till smooth. Put the peas through a fine mesh sieve to remove skins (of peas). Add salt & pepper to taste. Reheat in 350° oven for 15 min. till hot. Serve. ♥

# GREEN BEANS
# AND ONIONS

Serves Four

It's the wine vinegar that turns this into something special. 🧅

1 lb. young green beans
1 chopped onion
2 Tbsp. butter
salt and pepper
½ tsp. wine vinegar
finely chopped parsley

Snap off stems and tips of beans; leave them whole. Cook them in boiling water until tender, but still firm. Drain them. In a heavy saucepan slowly sauté the onion in the butter until soft and golden. Add the green beans, mix well, and reheat over low flame for a few minutes. Add salt and pepper to taste, then the vinegar. Sprinkle with chopped parsley before serving. ♥

"I am not a gourmet chick." ♥ Pearl Bailey

# CREAM CHEESE POTATOES

Serves Eight

I always make these for Thanksgiving ♥. If you have any leftovers, they'll keep in your refrigerator for 2 weeks and they are so good formed into patties, dipped in flour, and fried in butter ♥.

9 large potatoes, peeled and halved
2  3-oz. pkgs. cream cheese
1 c. sour cream
2 tsp. onion salt
1 tsp. salt
½ tsp. pepper
3 Tbsp. butter

Cook potatoes in boiling, salted water until tender. Mash them until smooth. Add the remaining ingredients and beat till light and fluffy ♥.

"I hate guests who complain of the cooking and leave bits and pieces all over the place and cream cheese sticking to the mirrors."

Colette, Chéri 1920 ♥

79

# TWICE-BAKED
# POTATOES

350° Serves Six

These potatoes can turn an ordinary meal into
something special with very little extra work. ♥

6 medium baking potatoes
1 8oz. pkg. cream cheese
½ c. hot milk
1 tsp. onion salt
2 Tbsp. butter
Freshly ground pepper
½ c. parsley, finely chopped
paprika

Put cream cheese out to soften. Scrub potatoes
and dry. Grease them with butter & salt the
skins. Bake at 350° for 1 hour. Remove from
oven & cool to handle. Cut them in half lengthwise ~ remove cooked potato to bowl, being care-
ful to reserve skins whole. Mash with cream
cheese, hot milk, onion salt, butter, & pepper. Pile
mixture back into skins. Sprinkle with paprika
& parsley & bake 20 min. more. ♥

# · PESTO ·

Makes Two Cups

Pesto, to me, is like "green gold". Here on the Vineyard I grow basil in the summer, make and freeze pesto to have all winter long. It is delicious on pasta, on sliced garden tomatoes, or in soups. For an appetizer I once hollowed out cherry tomatoes and filled them with pesto. ♥ ♥ ♥ ♥

2 c. fresh basil
3 Tbsp. pine nuts
2 cloves garlic
1/2 tsp. salt

dash of pepper
1/2 c. Parmesan cheese
1/4 c. Romano cheese
2/3 c. olive oil
2 Tbsp. butter

To prepare: Toast the pinenuts in a small skillet in a bit of butter. Cut the Parmesan & Romano into one-inch squares and grate separately in your food processor ~ measure out. Wash and drain basil ~ remove stems. Put all ingredients into food processor and blend until smooth. Freeze or refrigerate until ready to use. ♥

# POTATO CROQUETTES

350° Serves Six to Eight

To the true potato connoisseur, no amount of work is too much in the quest for potato perfection ♥.

| | |
|---|---|
| 8 med. russet potatoes | 4 slices bacon |
| 2 eggs, beaten | ½ c. onion, minced |
| 3 Tbsp. heavy cream | ½ c. milk |
| salt & pepper, to taste | 2 eggs, beaten |
| ¼ tsp. nutmeg | ½ c. unbleached flour |
| ½ c. cheddar cheese, grated | 3 c. bread crumbs |
| 2 Tbsp. chives, minced | oil for frying |
| 2 Tbsp. parsley, minced | sour cream |

Bake potatoes for 1 hour at 350°. Cool to handle. Scoop potato pulp into a large bowl & mash well. (Reserve skins for eating later!) Stir beaten eggs into potatoes & add cream to hold pulp together. Add salt, pepper, nutmeg, cheese, chives & parsley & stir well. Fry bacon till crisp (reserve grease); cool & crumble over potatoes. Pour out all but 1 Tbsp. bacon fat & sauté onion in fat, slowly, till soft. Add the onions to the potato mixture & stir well. Form the potatoes into little balls or cylinders. Mix together milk & eggs in a small bowl. Roll each croquette in flour; dip them in egg mixture & then into bread crumbs. Put about 1" oil into large skillet over med. high heat. Fry croquettes until well browned & put them on a cookie sheet. Bake them at 350° for about six minutes. Serve hot with sour cream on the side. ♥

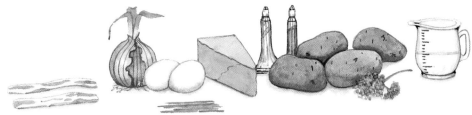

# FILLED TOMATOES

400° ♥ Serves six

They're crisped on top, the stuffing is moist and flavorful ~ and they go with almost everything. Perfect with fish, perfect with beef ~ even perfect with scrambled eggs for breakfast!

- 6 firm, ripe tomatoes
- 2 cloves mashed, minced garlic
- 5 Tbsp. minced parsley
- 4 Tbsp. minced green onion
- ¼ tsp. thyme
- ¼ tsp. salt
- freshly ground pepper
- ⅓ c. olive oil
- ¾ c. plain dry bread crumbs

Preheat oven to 400°. Cut the tomatoes in half and gently squeeze out the juice and seeds. Lightly salt and pepper the halves. Blend all remaining ingredients and taste to correct seasoning. Fill each tomato half & sprinkle with a few drops of olive oil. Arrange tomatoes in roasting pan, and bake in upper third of your oven for 12 minutes or until filling is golden brown. ♥ These can be made ahead and cooked when needed. ♥

# SPINACH SOUFFLÉ

350°  Serves Four

Wonderful texture and flavor ~ a good complement to an icy cold
Gazpacho with shrimp. ♥

1 c. cottage cheese
1 3oz. pkg. cream cheese, softened
2 eggs
3 Tbsp. flour
2 Tbsp. melted butter
3/4 tsp. salt
1/8 tsp. each nutmeg & pepper
1 10oz. pkg. spinach, thawed & drained

Place all ingredients except spinach in blender. Blend well.
Combine spinach with cheese mixture and pour into a buttered
quart soufflé dish. Set dish in a pan of hot water. Bake
in a 350° oven for 70 minutes, or until set in center. ♥

# Asian-Inspired
# SWEET POTATO

425°  Serves Two

So much healthy flavor, you won't need butter ~ but be sure to eat the crispy, crunchy, vitamin-rich skin. Makes the perfect "little dinner." Easy & fun to grow sweet potatoes in the garden.

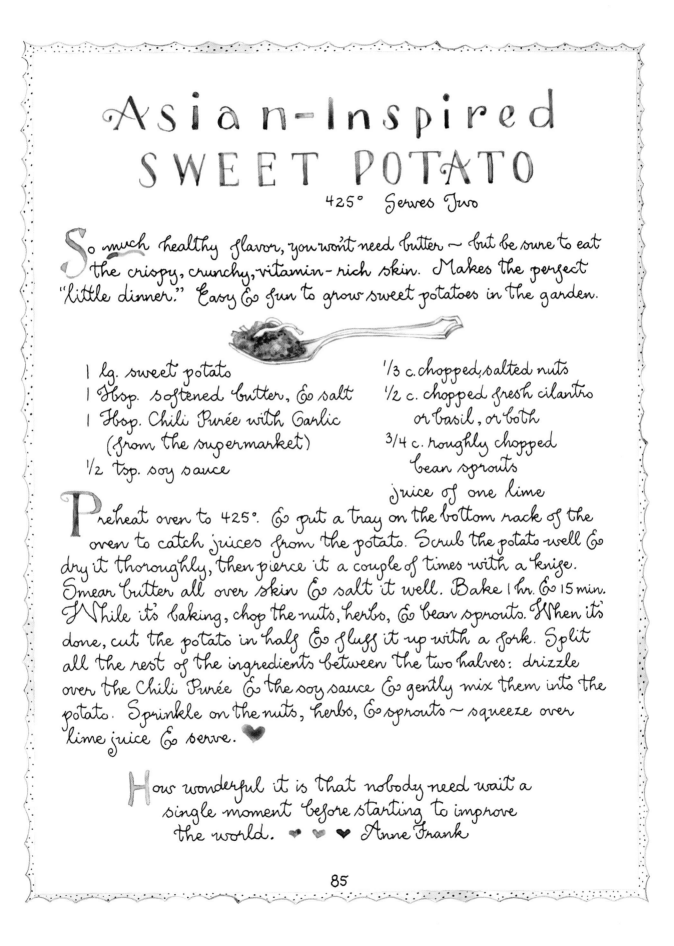

1 lg. sweet potato
1 Tbsp. softened butter, & salt
1 Tbsp. Chili Purée with Garlic
   (from the supermarket)
½ tsp. soy sauce

⅓ c. chopped, salted nuts
½ c. chopped fresh cilantro
   or basil, or both
¾ c. roughly chopped
   bean sprouts
juice of one lime

Preheat oven to 425°. & put a tray on the bottom rack of the oven to catch juices from the potato. Scrub the potato well & dry it thoroughly, then pierce it a couple of times with a knife. Smear butter all over skin & salt it well. Bake 1 hr. & 15 min. While it's baking, chop the nuts, herbs, & bean sprouts. When it's done, cut the potato in half & fluff it up with a fork. Split all the rest of the ingredients between the two halves: drizzle over the Chili Purée & the soy sauce & gently mix them into the potato. Sprinkle on the nuts, herbs, & sprouts ~ squeeze over lime juice & serve. ♥

How wonderful it is that nobody need wait a single moment before starting to improve the world. ♥ ♥ ♥ Anne Frank

# TOMATO CAULIFLOWER CASSEROLE

375° Serves Six

A hearty casserole with a lovely crusty topping. ♥

1 cauliflower washed & separated into bite~sized pieces
6 tomatoes peeled, seeded, & chopped
½ c. melted butter
freshly ground pepper
½ c. Parmesan cheese
⅓ c. bread crumbs
1 c. grated Muenster cheese
½ c. minced parsley

Preheat oven to 375°. Steam the cauliflower just until tender ~ reserve.
Dip each tomato into boiling water for about 35 seconds and peel
off the skin with your fingers. Cut them in half, squeeze out the
juice & seeds, and chop coarsely. Butter a casserole, put in the
cauliflower flowerets, layer the tomatoes on top, and pepper to
taste. Dribble half the butter over the top. Combine cheeses,
breadcrumbs, & parsley in a bowl & sprinkle evenly over casserole.
Dribble over remaining butter and bake 30 minutes until browned.
Serve hot. ♥

"The Greeks had just one word for 'economize'.
Our New England grandmothers had twelve:
'Eat it up; use it up; make do, or do without.' "
♥ Helen Adamson ♥

# CHILI CASSEROLE

350° Serves Six

A delicious dish to serve in a vegetarian dinner — perfect with Chicken Enchiladas (p.103). ♥

5 4oz. cans whole, mild green chiles
3 c. Jack cheese, thinly sliced
1 c. milk
4 eggs

3 Tbsp. unbleached flour
freshly ground pepper
3 c. Cheddar cheese, grated
2 Tbsp. parsley or cilantro

Preheat oven to 350°. Slit chilies open & mop with paper towels to remove excess moisture. Stuff each chili with a slice of Jack cheese & place them in ungreased baking dish. Whisk together milk, eggs, flour & pepper to taste and pour over chilies. Sprinkle grated cheese over the top & bake 45 min. Remove from oven, sprinkle minced parsley or cilantro over the casserole & Serve. ♥

# POTATO PACKAGES

350° Serves Six

These are great to serve at barbecues — Everyone gets a package. ♥

6 lg. baking potatoes, cubed
12 Tbsp. chopped onion
6 Tbsp. minced parsley

6 Tbsp. heavy cream
6 Tbsp. butter
salt & pepper to taste

Preheat oven to 350°. Lay out 6 large pieces of aluminum foil & evenly divide potatoes among them. Sprinkle each with 2 Tbsp. onion, 1 Tbsp. parsley, 1 Tbsp. cream. Dot each with 1 Tbsp. butter; s & p to taste. Wrap tightly — put on cookie sheet; bake 45 min. Serve. ♥

"Like a good pioneer, Father hankered to eat outdoors. And he ate outdoors, come gale, come zephyr. . . . Outdoors put an edge on my Father like that on a new-filed saw. . . .

"Beyond the cook-house, under the oaks that dipped their eastern leaves in the ocean, Father built him a table, with benches all the way around it, and mother had to serve our meals there. The wind blew up the tablecloth. We had to anchor it down with big stones. Things cooled off. The tea went flat and chilled. Ants got into the sugar. Fuzzy caterpillars dropped into our milk. Bees got into the syrup and into Father's trousers. Bees stung Father. But eat out under the sky he would. . . .

"I can see Father and all of us out there under the oaks even yet. A dozen of us round one table. Girls with honey-colored hair flowing in the wind, little boys' spiralled curls ruffling up. Golden bumble bees blazing past. A stiff breeze up. Butterflies lighting on the rim of the milk-pitcher. The sunlight making polka dots on our noses and the tablecloth, as it spilled down through the oak leaves. The whole deep sky blue above us, dappled with fair-weather clouds. . . . Seagulls leaning white on the wind. And Father with his big brown moustache all one way in the wind, the wind in his blue eyes, making them twinkle. Father smiling and eating hugely and shouting out between mouthfuls —
"Yes, Sir! This is the way to live! Out in the air, out where a man belongs!""

Robert P. Tristram Coffin ♥

MAIN DISHES

"Several years ago 'Life' had a picture story on how to skin an eel . . . . I trust everyone cut it out and put it in his files."

♥ James Beard ♥

# COLD SALMON WITH WATERCRESS AIOLI

Serves Six

A beautiful make-ahead dish ~ the colors are subtle, the flavors delightful. Serve it with Spring Medley (p.74). ♥

1 whole egg
2 egg yolks
3 Tbsp. fresh lemon juice
2 tsp. Dijon mustard
2 cloves garlic
½ c. olive oil

½ c. vegetable oil
½ c. watercress, leaves only
½ c. fresh dill
Freshly ground pepper & salt, to taste
2½ lbs. fresh salmon

Put the egg, egg yolks, lemon juice, mustard & garlic into food processor & blend 1 minute. Blend the olive & vegetable oils together, then, with machine running, pour in the oil in a very slow steady stream. Add watercress & dill to sauce & whirl to blend well ~ sauce will be light green. Add freshly ground pepper & salt to taste. Chill. Remove skin & bones from salmon (tweezers work very well for the bones). Place the salmon on a rack set into a large skillet with a cover. Add about an inch of water to the pan, cover & steam about 10 min. till fish begins to flake. Remove to your refrigerator & chill. When ready, put salmon on serving plates, spoon over about 3~4 Tbsp. of sauce for each & serve. ♥

90

# HERB ROASTED CHICKEN

425° Serves Four

A heavenly roasted chicken flavored with herbs; brown, juicy, and crisp-skinned. Serve with Potato Croquettes (p.82) and, for dessert, luscious Baked Bananas (p.162). ♥

1 large roasting chicken
3 Tbsp. butter, softened
1 clove garlic, minced
3 Tbsp. grated Parmesan
½ tsp. sage leaves

3/4 tsp. thyme leaves
3/4 tsp. basil leaves

6 Tbsp. butter, softened
salt

Preheat oven to 425°. Wash chicken inside & out; pat dry. Cream together 3 Tbsp. butter, garlic, Parmesan, sage, thyme and basil. This mixture goes under the skin, so turn the chicken breast-side-up and work your fingers under skin at the openings on each side of the breast. Continue onto thigh and leg & make the skin as loose as possible. Using fingers, spread herb mixture evenly under skin. Smear 3 Tbsp. butter both inside the chicken & on the outside of the skin. Put the chicken, breast up, in a roasting pan and then into the oven. Melt remaining butter; Cook chicken 15 min., basting once. Lower heat to 350°. Roast for about 20 min. per lb., basting with melted butter every 10 min. Chicken is done when the leg moves easily in its socket, & juices are clear yellow when pierced with fork. Allow chicken to sit 10 min. before carving. Serve. ♥

# VEAL BIRDS

350° Serves Six

This is one of my favorite recipes for a special dinner. Try it with hot homemade applesauce — maybe for Valentines Day. ♥

2½ lbs. veal cutlets

2½ c. stuffing, your own, or p. 94

1½ Tbsp. oil

3 Tbsp. butter

freshly ground pepper

salt, to taste

2 c. chicken broth

½ lb. mushrooms, thickly sliced

3/4 c. heavy cream

5 slices bacon, crisply fried

Preheat oven to 350°. Trim fat off veal & pound with mallet till ¼" thick. Cut into pieces about 5" x 6". Put stuffing down the middle of each cutlet & roll into little packages; tie with string. Melt oil & butter in large skillet and brown birds very quickly. Put them in a single layer into a casserole, surround with sliced mushrooms, pour chicken broth over, cover tightly, and bake 35 min. Pour in the cream, remove the cover, and bake 30 min. more. Remove from oven, sprinkle on crumbled bacon, and serve. ♥ For applesauce recipe see page 155. ♥

REAL BIRDS

92

# FILET MIGNON IN PHYLLO WITH MADEIRA SAUCE

### 400° Serves Six

This makes a gorgeous presentation in the beautifully browned phyllo. ♥

3 lbs. filet mignon steaks, 2" thick
4 Tbsp. butter
1 lb. mushrooms, minced & <u>dried</u>
4 shallots, minced
1 pkg. phyllo pastry
½ c. butter, melted
Madeira Sauce (recipe below)

The Victim

Preheat oven to 400°. Trim the fat off the meat. Quickly brown the filets in 2 Tbsp. butter over high heat. Set aside. Melt remaining butter in the same pan & sauté the mushrooms & shallots for 4-5 min., till soft. Remove from heat. Layer 12 sheets of phyllo together, brushing each layer with melted butter. (Phyllo dries out quickly~ keep unused portion covered.) Spread ½ the mushroom mixture on pastry & put the beef on top. Cover beef with remaining mushrooms. Fold the phyllo around the beef. Prepare 6 more sheets of pastry; brush each with butter. Seal all edges with additional pastry & brush top with butter. Place beef in buttered baking pan & bake for 30 min. till pastry is browned. Serve with:

## Madeira Sauce

3 Tbsp. butter
1½ Tbsp. flour
3/4 c. beef stock

1 tsp. Kitchen Bouquet, for color (opt.)
¼ c. Madeira wine
freshly ground pepper

Melt butter, stir in flour, cook 5 min. Add beef stock, Kitchen Bouquet & Madeira. Cook until thickened; stir in pepper to taste. ♥

93

# APPLES, SWEET POTATOES, WITH PORK CHOPS

### 400° Serves Six

The wonderful thing about this recipe is that your whole delicious dinner is made in one dish. ♥ It's perfect for a cold wintry day ♥.

6 lg. sweet potatoes
4 Tbsp. cooking oil
6 2" thick pork chops
salt and pepper

Stuffing
6 lg. tart apples
1 c. golden raisins
1 tsp. cinnamon

Preheat oven to 400°. Peel the potatoes; cut them into large chunks & boil them till they're about half-done. Set aside. Heat the oil and brown the chops quickly on both sides ~ salt & pepper. Remove and cool. Make the stuffing. Cut a deep slit in the side of each chop & fill with the stuffing. Put the stuffed chops & the sweet potatoes into a large baking pan. Peel, halve & core the apples. Place them in the pan with the chops & potatoes & sprinkle on the raisins. Sprinkle cinnamon on each apple. Cover the pan tightly with foil and bake 50 minutes until apples & chops are tender. ♥

## Stuffing

1 cube butter
1 med. onion, finely chopped
3 ribs celery, chopped
½ c. parsley, minced
2 c. dry bread crumbs
salt and pepper
♥

Melt butter ~ add onion and celery and cook slowly till soft. Add parsley, bread crumbs, and salt & pepper. Mix well and correct consistency with more bread crumbs or butter. ♥

# ORIENTAL FISH

Serves Four

Tender fish filets steamed in an Asian sauce. ♥ Quick & easy — low-calorie & delicious. ♥

4 fish filets: flounder, sole, yellow tail
1 carrot, julienned
3 green onions with tops, julienned
    fresh ginger, to taste
2 Tbsp. parsley, minced (or 1 Tbsp. cilantro)
2 Tbsp. rice vinegar
2 Tbsp. light soy sauce
1 Tbsp. lemon juice
2 tsp. sesame oil

Lay the filets on a heat-proof plate — spread vegies over the top. Mix together vinegar, soy sauce, lemon juice & sesame oil; pour mixture over the fish. Into a large deep skillet put a Pyrex lid or another heat-proof plate — something the fish plate can sit on & be off the bottom. Add an inch or so of water to the skillet. Put the plate of fish into the pan. Cover & steam 7-10 min. Serve. ♥ You can also roll the vegies up in the filets & cook them that way. ♥ Try fresh snow peas & steamed new potatoes with this dish. ♥

"Take time for all things".
♥ Benjamin Franklin ♥

# PASTA WITH SMOKED SALMON & PEAS

### Serves Six

Light and summery ~ delicate flavors and colors blended to a delightful taste and texture. ♥ Serve the pasta with a crisp salad & Blueberry Angel Food Cake (p. 137) for dessert. ♥ Trust me, they'll love it ~ and you!

3/4 c. dry white wine
4 Tbsp. shallots, minced
1 1/4 c. heavy cream
8 oz. narrow egg noodles, dried

3/4 c. cooked peas
3 Tbsp. fresh dill, snipped
1/3 lb. smoked salmon, sliced
4 Tbsp. pine nuts, toasted

Toast the pine nuts in a small skillet with a Tbsp. of butter. Keep your eye on them ~ they burn easily. Set aside on paper towel to drain. Cook the peas & set aside. Put the white wine & shallots together in a small saucepan & bring to boil. Allow the wine to reduce by about a Tbsp. Stir in cream; bring to boil; simmer for 5~6 min. Cover the pan & remove from heat. Put the pasta into boiling water & cook just till tender; rinse in cool water; drain. Put the pasta into serving dish. Bring sauce back to boil ~ remove from heat ~ stir in peas & dill. Pour sauce over pasta; toss to coat. Add the thinly sliced strips of smoked salmon & the freshly toasted pine nuts ~ Toss gently & serve. ♥

♥ ♥ ♥

"We live in deeds, not years; in thoughts, not breaths; In feelings, not in figures on a dial. We should count time by heart-throbs. He most lives who thinks most ~ feels the noblest ~ acts the best."

P. J. Bailey ♥

# PAN-FRIED CHICKEN
# & CREAM GRAVY

Serves Four

Indulge yourself for an old-time Sunday dinner. Have it at four o'clock on a nippy fall day and don't forget the mashed potatoes, ♥ hot biscuits with butter and honey ~ Delicious!   For Best Biscuits recipe, see p. 154.

For Best Biscuits recipe, see p. 154.

3 lb. chicken in 8 pieces          1 tsp. salt
Milk                               ½ tsp. pepper
1 c. flour                         Frying oil

Wash and dry the chicken pieces. Put in a shallow dish with milk to cover for 1 hour. Mix the flour, salt and pepper in a plastic bag. Drop the milk ~ soaked chicken in the bag and shake well. Heat ½ inch oil in large skillet to medium ~ high and put the dark meat in first. Five minutes later add the white meat and fry for 25 minutes, turning often with tongs. Remove, drain on paper towels and keep warm while you make the:

### Cream Gravy

3 Tbsp. pan drippings and butter      1½ c. cream
3 Tbsp. flour                         salt and pepper

Heat the pan drippings and butter and scrape up any brown bits in the pan. Stir in the flour and blend, over low heat. Slowly add cream, stirring constantly, until smooth. Add salt & pepper; cook 7 minutes.

# RICE AND SOUR CREAM CASSEROLE

350° Serves Six

This is a wonderful dish to serve to your vegetarian friends, healthy and filling. The cheese makes a good crusty top. ♥

1 c. uncooked brown rice
3 med. zucchini, sliced
1 7½ oz. can chopped green chilies
12 oz. jack cheese, grated
2 lg. tomatoes, thinly sliced
2 c. sour cream

1 tsp. oregano
1 tsp. garlic salt
¼ c. chopped green pepper
¼ c. chopped green onion
2 Tbsp. chopped fresh parsley

Cook the rice. Layer in large buttered casserole: cooked rice, chopped chilies, ½ of the cheese, zucchini and tomato slices. Combine the sour cream, oregano, garlic salt, green pepper, and green onion. Spoon this mixture over the tomatoes and sprinkle on the rest of the cheese. Bake at 350° for 45 minutes. Sprinkle with fresh parsley. Serve either as main course or as a side dish. ♥

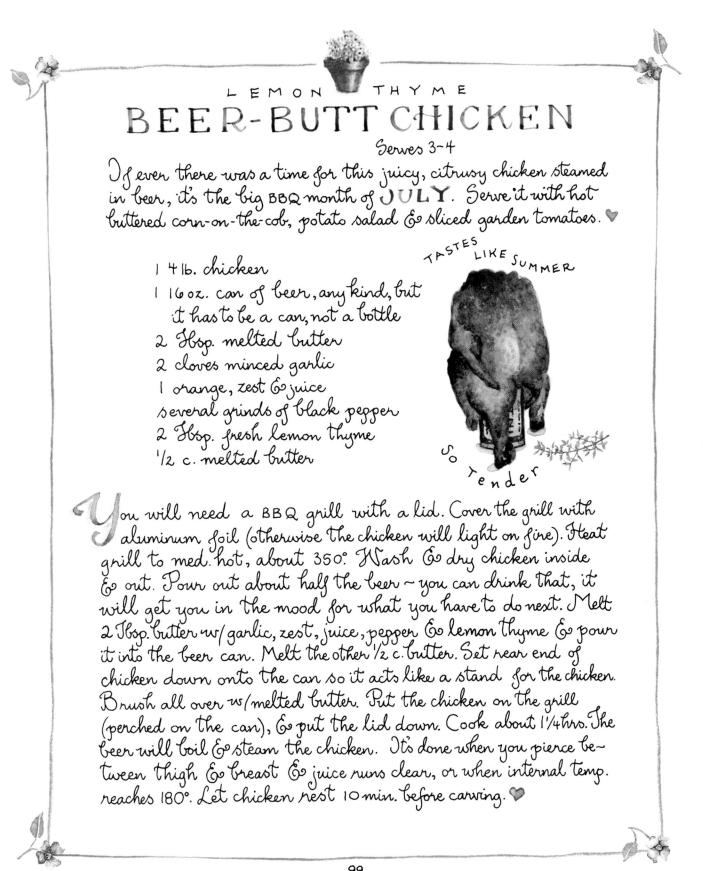

# LEMON THYME
# BEER-BUTT CHICKEN
### Serves 3-4

If ever there was a time for this juicy, citrusy chicken steamed in beer, it's the big BBQ month of JULY. Serve it with hot buttered corn-on-the-cob, potato salad & sliced garden tomatoes. 🖤

1 4 lb. chicken
1 16 oz. can of beer, any kind, but
   it has to be a can, not a bottle
2 Tbsp. melted butter
2 cloves minced garlic
1 orange, zest & juice
several grinds of black pepper
2 Tbsp. fresh lemon thyme
½ c. melted butter

*TASTES LIKE SUMMER*

*So Tender*

You will need a BBQ grill with a lid. Cover the grill with aluminum foil (otherwise the chicken will light on fire). Heat grill to med. hot, about 350°. Wash & dry chicken inside & out. Pour out about half the beer ~ you can drink that, it will get you in the mood for what you have to do next. Melt 2 Tbsp. butter w/garlic, zest, juice, pepper & lemon thyme & pour it into the beer can. Melt the other ½ c. butter. Set near end of chicken down onto the can so it acts like a stand for the chicken. Brush all over w/melted butter. Put the chicken on the grill (perched on the can), & put the lid down. Cook about 1¼ hrs. The beer will boil & steam the chicken. It's done when you pierce between thigh & breast & juice runs clear, or when internal temp. reaches 180°. Let chicken rest 10 min. before carving. 🖤

# CHICKEN BREASTS STUFFED with CHEESE

Serves Six 375°

Use plump breasts so you can get lots of cheese inside! This is such a favorite with one of my friends ~ he requests it every chance he gets. ♥

3 large chicken breasts, boned & halved
1 lb. jack cheese, sliced
4 eggs
3 Tbsp. minced parsley
3 Tbsp. freshly grated Parmesan cheese
salt & pepper
½ c. unbleached flour
4 Tbsp. olive oil
juice of ½ lemon

Preheat oven to 375°. Carefully put a slit in the side of each breast-half with a sharp knife. Fill with as many slices of jack cheese as will comfortably fit. Fasten tightly with toothpicks so the cheese won't melt out while cooking. Mix together eggs, Parmesan cheese, and parsley. Roll the chicken in flour, coating heavily, and then dip in the egg mixture. Heat the oil in a large skillet over moderately high heat. Put the chicken in and pour the rest of the egg mixture over the top. Fry very quickly just to lightly brown. Place chicken in buttered baking pan ~ lay any extra cheese on tops and around sides of chicken. Bake 25 min. ~ do not overcook. Remove toothpicks, squeeze lemon juice over, sprinkle on some parsley and serve. ♥

# LEMON CHICKEN

Serves Six

One of the easiest, fastest "gourmet" dishes I know.
These chicken breasts melt in your mouth.
Serve them with buttered peas & stuffed tomatoes.

3 whole chicken breasts, boned, skinned & halved
1½ c. unbleached flour
⅓ c. butter
2 Tbsp. olive oil
salt and pepper

Wash and dry chicken breasts. Pound them flat
with a mallet. Melt the butter and oil in a large
skillet. Put the flour in a plastic bag and drop the
breasts in to coat. Regulate the heat to moderately
high, and put the chicken breasts in the skillet.
Cook approx. 3 minutes on each side. When they
are done, salt & pepper them and put them on an
oven-proof dish and into a 250° oven to keep warm
while you make the sauce.

### The Sauce:

Add 4 Tbsp. butter to the chicken skillet & melt,
scraping up brown bits in pan. Remove from heat;
add 4 Tbsp. finely chopped parsley, & the juice from
½ lemon. Pour hot sauce over breasts and serve.

# SCALLOPS IN PUFF PASTRY

450° Serves Four

Asparagus & fresh scallops in scallop shells baked with a top crust of puff pastry & finished with Citrus Butter. ♥

1 bunch of asparagus
2 Tbsp. butter
2 Tbsp. sherry
4 large scallop shells

1½ lbs. scallops
about ½ lb. puff pastry
1 egg, beaten
Citrus Butter

Make Citrus Butter (recipe below). Preheat oven to 450° Break tough ends off asparagus & discard. Slice the spears into ½" diagonal pieces. Sauté them in butter for 2 min. over medium high heat. Add sherry & stir 1 min. more. Remove from heat & divide asparagus evenly between the 4 scallop shells ~ then divide the uncooked scallops between the shells. Roll out the puff pastry to ¼" thick. Lay a small plate on the dough & cut around to fit over scallop shells. Lay the circles of puff pastry over the shells & seal tightly over edges. Brush beaten egg over entire pastry, including edges. Bake 10~15 min. until golden brown. Cut open center & add a melon baller full of Citrus Butter ~ serve. ♥

# CITRUS BUTTER

½ c. butter, softened
juice of 1 lime
juice of 1 lemon

juice of ½ orange
1 tsp. each of julienne zest
of lime, lemon & orange

Blanche the zest (to take out the bitterness); strain. Cream all ingredients together; chill. ♥

SIMPLY THE BEST

# CHICKEN
# ENCHILADAS

### 350° Serves Six

Have "Mexican Night" at your house 🛸. Serve these delicious enchiladas with a Chili Casserole (p.87) and some refried beans with chopped onion and melted cheese. ♥ And don't forget the Margaritas! ♥

3 c. cooked chopped chicken
1 4 oz. can chopped green chilies
1 7 oz. can green chili salsa
3/4 tsp. salt

2½ c. heavy cream
1 doz. corn tortillas
2 c. grated Jack cheese
oil

Preheat oven to 350°. Mix together chicken, green chilies, & green chili salsa. In another fairly large bowl mix together cream and salt. Heat about 1 inch of oil in a small frying pan. Dip each tortilla into hot oil for about 3 seconds, just to soften. Drain on paper towels and lay into bowl containing cream. Fill each tortilla with chicken mixture ~ roll them up and place into ungreased baking dish. Pour extra cream over the enchiladas and sprinkle on the cheese. Bake uncovered for 25 minutes and serve hot. 🛸

103

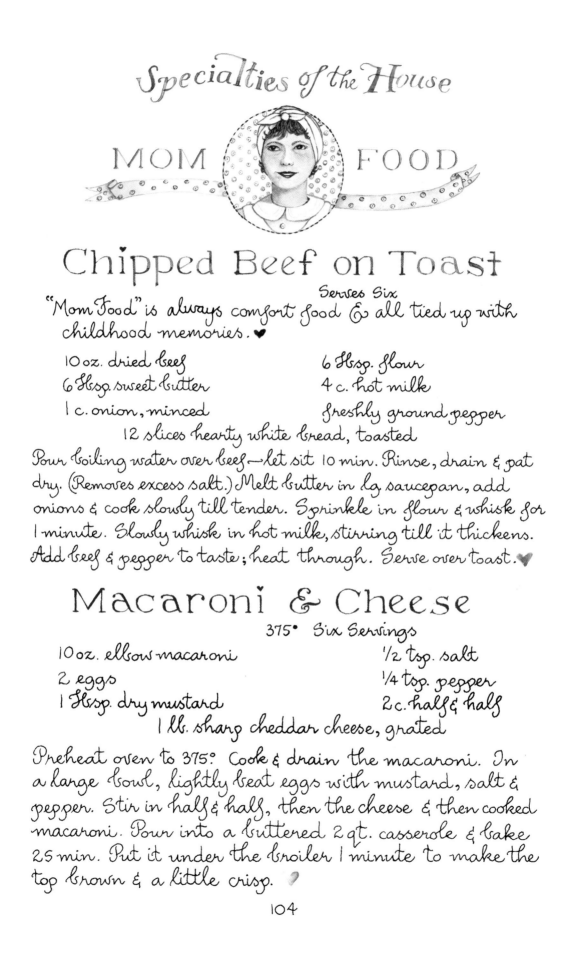

# Specialties of the House

## MOM FOOD

# Chipped Beef on Toast

Serves Six

"Mom Food" is always comfort food & all tied up with childhood memories. ♥

10 oz. dried beef
6 Tbsp. sweet butter
1 c. onion, minced

6 Tbsp. flour
4 c. hot milk
freshly ground pepper

12 slices hearty white bread, toasted

Pour boiling water over beef—let sit 10 min. Rinse, drain & pat dry. (Removes excess salt.) Melt butter in lg saucepan, add onions & cook slowly till tender. Sprinkle in flour & whisk for 1 minute. Slowly whisk in hot milk, stirring till it thickens. Add beef & pepper to taste; heat through. Serve over toast. ♥

# Macaroni & Cheese

375° Six Servings

10 oz. elbow macaroni
2 eggs
1 Tbsp. dry mustard

½ tsp. salt
¼ tsp. pepper
2 c. half & half

1 lb. sharp cheddar cheese, grated

Preheat oven to 375°. Cook & drain the macaroni. In a large bowl, lightly beat eggs with mustard, salt & pepper. Stir in half & half, then the cheese & then cooked macaroni. Pour into a buttered 2 qt. casserole & bake 25 min. Put it under the broiler 1 minute to make the top brown & a little crisp.

# SPARERIBS & JUICE ♥

### 275° Serves Four

My mom called us "wild Indians" sometimes, & never did we look the part more than when we were devouring her wonderful spareribs & juice. She has a picture of us all around the table during one of these feasts ~ my poor dad has a look on his face that clearly says "Must you take a picture NOW?" But the rest of us are smiling, with enough "juice" on our faces, hands & clothes to make a whole other dinner. This was an often-requested birthday dinner & was served with garden corn on the cob dripping with butter & fluffy mashed potatoes WITH lumps. For dessert ~ watermelon ~ served curbside ♥.

Pork ribs for four
2 c. pineapple juice
½ c. catsup
2 Tbsp. steak sauce
2 Tbsp. brown sugar
1 Tbsp. white vinegar
1 tsp. ground mustard
3 cloves minced garlic (opt.)

Put the ribs in a roasting pan & into a 275° oven for 2 hours. Pour off fat. Mix together all remaining ingredients & pour over the ribs. Bake 1 hour more. Serve in a large bowl surrounded with juice. ♥

The grand essentials of happiness are: something to do, something to give, something to love & something to hope for. ♥

# CORNISH GAME HENS
350° Serves Four

Wild rice, toasted nuts, a hint of orange, & sweet hoisin sauce make for interesting flavors & textures — the marinade browns beautifully♥.

| | |
|---|---|
| ¼ c. sherry | ¾ c. wild rice |
| ½ c. hoisin sauce | 1½ c. chicken broth |
| 3 Tbsp. toasted sesame oil | ½ c. hazelnuts |
| zest of 1 orange, blanched | 3 Tbsp. butter |
| 2 large game hens | 2 shallots, chopped |

Mix together sherry, hoisin sauce, sesame oil & the blanched zest of an orange, minced. (Blanching removes bitterness.) Wash & dry the hens. Rub the mixture all over birds, inside & out. Pour remaining mixture over hens — cover & refrigerate for at least 3 hours (overnight is O.K.) Periodically brush the birds with marinade. About 2 hours before you plan to serve, simmer the rice in chicken broth for about 45 min., till tender. Meanwhile put the nuts on a cookie sheet & toast them in a 350° oven for about 30 min., till browned. Chop very coarsely. Melt butter in heavy skillet; add shallots & toasted nuts. Sauté slowly until butter is browned (not blackened); add rice, stir for about 2 min. & remove from heat. Stuff the hens with rice mixture; place them breast side up in baking dish & bake at 350° for 45~50 min. Mix remaining marinade with remaining rice — put mixture in buttered baking dish & then into oven for last 15 min. of baking time. Split the hens & serve them on a bed of rice. ♥

# PAUPIETTES WITH BEURRE BLANC

400°    Serves Six

When you unmold these you have a perfect little circle of steamed fish wrapped around a center of spinach stuffing. Sauced over lightly with the beurre blanc & served with Glazed Carrots (p.73) they make a pretty delectable picture. ♥ Try Tomato Soup (p.36) to start & Cheesecake (p.121) for dessert. ♥

2 c. fresh spinach, blanched
10 mushrooms, chopped
1 onion, finely chopped
2 cloves garlic, minced

6 Tbsp. butter
freshly ground pepper
dash nutmeg
1½ lbs. filets of flounder

Preheat oven to 400° Finely chop the blanched spinach & set aside. Sauté mushrooms, onion & garlic in 3 Tbsp. butter; add pepper to taste & just a pinch of nutmeg; cook, stirring, till butter melts; remove from heat. Butter six 6 oz. ramekins. Score the darker side of the fish with a sharp knife & cut into pieces to line the ramekins, putting the scored side toward the inside Fill lined ramekins with spinach mixture. Cover with foil & place them in roasting pan. Pour boiling water into roasting pan ~ about 1" deep. Bake for 16 minutes. Remove from oven; drain off juices from ramekins and unmold onto serving dishes. Cover lightly with beurre blanc. ♥

## Beurre Blanc

¼ c. dry white wine
¼ c. white wine vinegar
3 Tbsp. shallots, chopped

1½ c. COLD butter
2 Tbsp. parsley, minced
salt & pepper, to taste

Boil wine, vinegar & shallots; reduce to 1~2 Tbsp. Turn heat VERY low. Whisking constantly, slowly add COLD butter, one Tbsp. at a time. Sauce will thicken ~ add parsley, salt & pepper. Pour over paupiettes. ♥

# LINGUINI IN WHITE CLAM SAUCE

Serves four

You can keep the ingredients for this easy dish in your pantry ~ and you'll always be ready for unexpected guests. ♥ Try it with a spinach salad (p.53), garlic bread (p.66) & steamed baby carrots. ♥ ♥ This dish can be used as a side dish for something extra special. ♥

½ c. butter
¼ c. olive oil
2 cloves garlic, minced
2 7½ oz. cans chopped clams
1 bottle clam juice
½ c. finely chopped parsley
½ lb. linguini, fresh is best
1 doz. fresh small clams, opt.
freshly grated Parmesan cheese

Heat butter and oil, add garlic and cook slowly until golden. Drain the clams ~ reserve the liquid and add enough bottled clam juice to make 2 cups. Stir the liquid into the butter mixture and simmer, uncovered, for 10 minutes. Add chopped clams, parsley, & salt and pepper & heat through. Cook the linguini in boiling water till just tender. Pour the sauce over. If using fresh clams (a nice touch, but not necessary) boil a small amount of water, add clams, cover, and steam just until they open. Arrange them around pasta and pour the sauce over all. Pass the Parmesan cheese and enjoy ♥. Tips: When you buy clams or mussels, make sure the shells are tightly closed. The best Parmeson cheese is Reggiano, expensive ~ but, do a taste test! ♥

# HEARTY DINNER STEW
## with buttered noodles

325° Serves 4

A cozy stew for a chilly night with flavors of orange, sweet potatoes, red wine, nutmeg, and raisins. ♥

2 Tbsp. flour
1 tsp. salt
½ tsp. pepper
3 lbs. lean beef chuck
2 Tbsp. olive oil
1 bottle of red wine
1 c. water
3 oz. tomato paste
1 med. onion in 1" dice
3 med. parsnips, peeled, in 1" pieces (or 5 carrots)

1 lg. sweet potato, peeled, in 1" pieces
zest of 1 orange
¼ c. fresh orange juice
2 bay leaves
¼ tsp. cayenne
¼ tsp. nutmeg
½ c. raisins
8 oz. wide egg noodles
2 Tbsp. butter
½ c. chopped parsley

Preheat oven to 325°. In a lg. bowl, mix flour, salt, & pepper. Cut beef into bite-sized pieces; cut off & discard fat. Put beef in bowl & coat well w/ flour mixture. Heat oil in lg., heavy, oven-proof pot with lid. In batches, quickly brown beef, transfer to plate. When all is done, deglaze pan w/ wine, scraping up brown bits. Stir in water, tomato paste, vegetables, zest & o.j., seasonings & raisins. Add beef to pot & bring to boil. Cover, put in oven for 2 hrs. Just before stew is done, cook the noodles; toss w/ butter & parsley. Remove bay leaves from stew before serving. ♥

# MY GRANDMA'S
# TURKEY STUFFING

### For a 20 lb. bird

I guess you could say this is the old-fashioned way to make stuffing — my great-grandmother also made it this way ♥. It's so moist and you can change it any way you like with additions of your own, but we like it plain & simple. ♥

    2 loaves white bread, dried
    1 loaf wheat bread, dried
    2 sticks butter
    2 or 3 onions, chopped
    6 stalks celery, chopped
    1 jar sage leaves
    1 Tbsp. salt or to taste
    freshly ground pepper

Set the bread out to dry a couple of days before you make the stuffing. ♥ Put about 6 in. of the hottest water you can stand to touch into your clean sink. Dip each slice of bread into the water; wring it out well & put it into a large bowl. The bread will be kind of chunky, doughy, chewy — melt butter in a large skillet. Very slowly, sauté the onions & celery in the butter until soft — do not brown the butter. Meanwhile, over the sink, rub the sage leaves between your fingers & remove woody stems — put the leaves in with the bread. Pour the butter mixture over the bread & mix well with your hands (but don't burn yourself!). Add about 1 Tbsp. salt — it needs lots of salt, so they say ♥, & then add pepper to taste. Now for the tasting, the tasting always goes on forever ♥ . . . is it right? More salt? More sage? More butter? So taste, and don't worry — we've never measured a thing & it's always delicious! Makes great sandwiches with sliced turkey & cranberry sauce ♥.

# SUMMER LOBSTER BOIL
# AT THE BEACH

"Summering" on Martha's Vineyard is a tradition with many
New England families; the clambake is another tradition.
I was new to the East Coast, had never been to a clambake,
but I was somehow put in charge of putting together a
clambake for fourteen people! And I was just getting over
the "I have to cut the oysters in half so I can get used to
them" stage! I looked through my (West Coast) cookbooks,
but found nothing on a clambake, so I decided to do my
own version ~ a lobster boil! It came together so beauti~
fully & was so much fun, that I would do it again in
a minute ~ here's what you'll need:

4-wheel-drive truck
2 shovels
wood, lots of it
a large rack from your oven or BBQ
a long board to walk on
large metal bucket or bowl
1 medium-sized metal trash can,
    brand new, with lid
a few rocks, like about 15
fresh water to drink
clam knife, sharp knife
large trash bags
large potholders
paper towels
toilet paper

short-legged beachchairs
flashlight
warm clothes, blankets to sit on
camera
wet washcloths in Tupperware
charcoal
lighter fluid, matches
long tongs
cheesecloth
large heavy paper plates
napkins, forks, cups
butter pots
lobster picks, crackers
beer, wine, soft drinks, coffee
cooler
ghost stories

# Menu

Iced littleneck clams on the half shell with horseradish sauce
Steamer clams with melted butter
Live lobsters, 1½ lbs. each      ♥ Condiments:
Roasted corn on the cob      lemon slices
Potato packages (recipe, p. 87)      horseradish sauce
Cheesecake (recipe, p. 121)      1 lb. of butter for melting

# To Do Ahead

Make cheesecake, chill, and cover tightly with plastic wrap. Make up one package of potatoes per person. Butter, salt & pepper ears of corn; wrap individually in tin foil ~ 1 or 2 per person. Order lobsters, littlenecks, steamers & ice to be picked up on the way to the beach. Slice lemons, make horseradish sauce (catsup, horse~radish, lemon juice, to taste), put cubes of butter into old saucepan for melting ~ make all beach-proof. Put cold drinks into cooler. Make coffee & fill thermos. Plan for cream & sugar. ♥

# Let's Go!

Load up the truck. Put the metal bucket upside-down in the bottom of the trash can (so that lobsters won't go to the bottom). Pick up the ice, fill the cooler & fill the trash can about half-way. Pick up lobsters & clams; put them on top of the ice in the can, cover and go merrily to the beach.

Drive right onto the beach and park for wind-break if necessary. Dig a small hole, circle with rocks, fill with charcoal, put grill on top, and light ~ this is for the potatoes & corn. Dig a big hole, fill it with wood, lay the long board across the hole ~ you'll need this board to walk on so that you can get close to the steaming lobsters without falling into the hole. Light the fire. When you're ready, remove the lobsters & clams from the trash~ can ~ dump out about ½ the ice (use for drinks) but leave the bucket in the can. Put the can on the fire to boil (lid on). Open the icy littleneck clams and serve them raw with horseradish sauce & lemon wedges. When the water is boil~ ing, melt some butter. Put the steamer clams into the cheesecloth & hang them inside the can until they open. Serve them with melted butter for dipping. Put the potatoes on the grill; cook for ½ hour. Drop lobsters in boiling water; steam for 15~20 min. Put the corn on the grill for about 8 min. Each person gets a lobster, a package of potatoes, corn on the cob, & a little pot of melted butter ~ pass the picks & lobster crackers. At the end, there's cheesecake & hot coffee.♥ And don't forget those nice wet washcloths you brought along.♥

## The End

We had such a wonderful time ~ we saw the sun drop into the sea, as the moon peeped through the beach grass behind us. One of our company had taken a trip to the library, where he'd boned up on some great ghost stories ~ & we sang all the words to all the songs anyone could remember. The fire was glowing, the moon was big & bright. It was a fabulous evening for all.♥

# EASTER EGG COLORING PARTY

This party has turned out to be an Easter Eve tradition and our celebration of Spring ~ its so much fun to be gathered around a table together talking & painting eggs ~ creativity abounds ♥.

What you'll need :

blown eggs                              paper napkins
small paintbrushes                  sharp pencils
watercolor paints                     3 or 4 jars of fresh
small jars of water                     clear nail polish

To blow out the eggs, prick a deep hole in each end of the egg with a needle. Put your mouth over one of the holes & blow hard till the egg comes out ~ it gets easier as the egg starts coming. This should be done before the party starts. Distribute brushes, pencils, etc. around the table ~ use the napkins to blot the brushes. The designs can be drawn (& erased) in pencil. Watercolors dry quickly. When completely dry, cover entire egg in clear nail polish. ♥ If your guests sign their eggs you can use them as place cards for Easter Dinner. ♥

"I remember the way we parted,
   The day and the way we met;
You hoped we were both brokenhearted,
   And knew we should both forget.
And the best and the worst of this is
   That neither is most to blame,
If you have forgotten my kisses
   And I have forgotten your name."
               A. C. Swinburne

"I thought that spring must last for ever more ~
For I was young, and loved, and it was May." ♥
Vera Brittain

D E S S E R T S

# CHAMPAGNE COCKTAILS

These are absolutely yummy ~ I like to serve them at a Christmas party, or to my girlfriends at a basket party or wedding shower. ♥ Contrary to one's first reaction, there is little chance of becoming addicted because the aftereffects can be totally devastating. But oh, what a night !

Chilled champagne glasses
Good-quality champagne
Sugar cubes
Angostura bitters

Soak the sugar cubes in the bitters. Drop one cube in each chilled champagne glass and fill with champagne. Serve. ♥

"Love is friendship set to music."
Anonymous ♥

# BLUEBERRY PIE

425°

I feel so lucky because my little house on the Vineyard is surrounded by wild blueberry bushes. ♥ And this recipe is a delicious result. I also freeze them so we can have pies in the winter ~ so if you don't have them fresh in your area, frozen ones are fine. ♥

Pie crust dough for two~crust 8" pie (p.129)
4 c. blueberries (if frozen, it's not necessary to defrost)
3/4 c. sugar
3½ Tbsp. flour
pinch of salt
squeeze of fresh lemon juice
1 Tbsp. butter

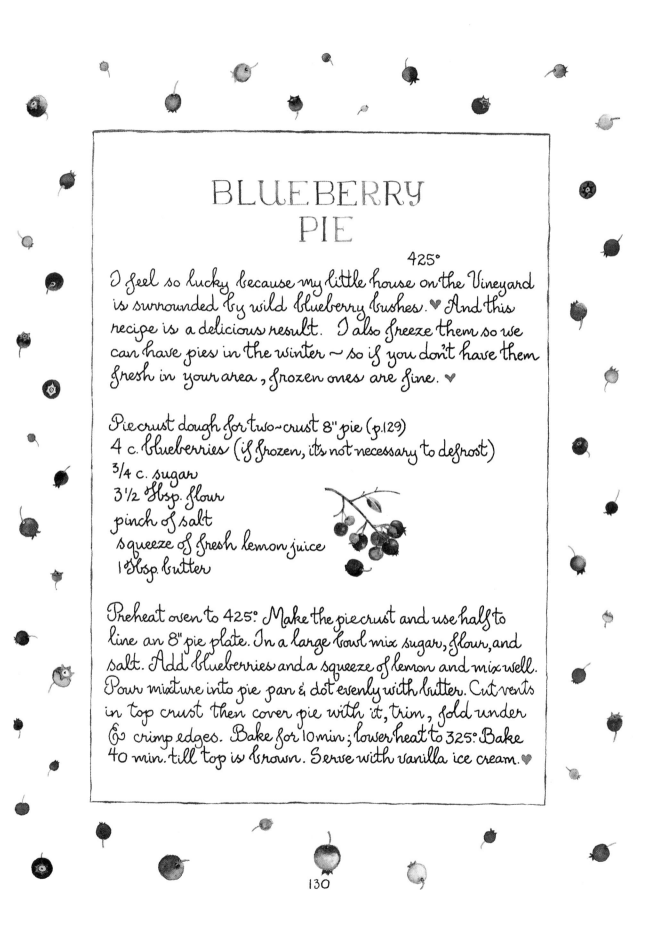

Preheat oven to 425° Make the pie crust and use half to line an 8" pie plate. In a large bowl mix sugar, flour, and salt. Add blueberries and a squeeze of lemon and mix well. Pour mixture into pie pan & dot evenly with butter. Cut vents in top crust then cover pie with it, trim, fold under & crimp edges. Bake for 10 min; lower heat to 325° Bake 40 min. till top is brown. Serve with vanilla ice cream. ♥

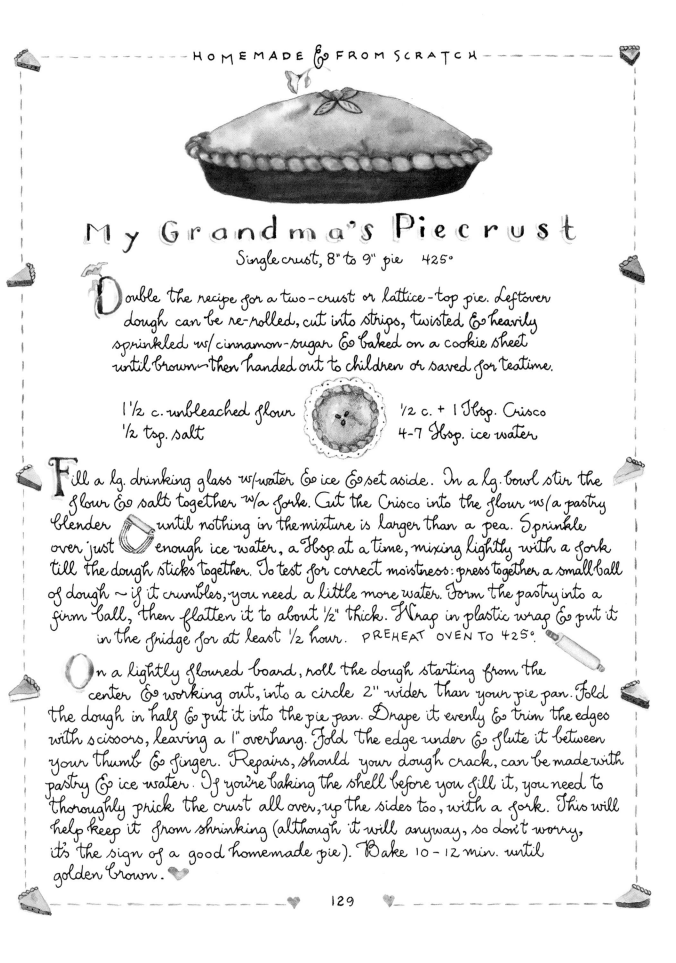

# My Grandma's Piecrust

Single crust, 8" to 9" pie    425°

Double the recipe for a two-crust or lattice-top pie. Leftover dough can be re-rolled, cut into strips, twisted & heavily sprinkled w/ cinnamon-sugar & baked on a cookie sheet until brown—then handed out to children or saved for teatime.

1½ c. unbleached flour          ½ c. + 1 Tbsp. Crisco
½ tsp. salt                     4-7 Tbsp. ice water

Fill a lg. drinking glass w/ water & ice & set aside. In a lg. bowl stir the flour & salt together w/ a fork. Cut the Crisco into the flour w/ a pastry blender until nothing in the mixture is larger than a pea. Sprinkle over just enough ice water, a Tbsp. at a time, mixing lightly with a fork till the dough sticks together. To test for correct moistness: press together a small ball of dough — if it crumbles, you need a little more water. Form the pastry into a firm ball, then flatten it to about ½" thick. Wrap in plastic wrap & put it in the fridge for at least ½ hour.    PREHEAT OVEN TO 425°.

On a lightly floured board, roll the dough starting from the center & working out, into a circle 2" wider than your pie pan. Fold the dough in half & put it into the pie pan. Drape it evenly & trim the edges with scissors, leaving a 1" overhang. Fold the edge under & flute it between your thumb & finger. Repairs, should your dough crack, can be made with pastry & ice water. If you're baking the shell before you fill it, you need to thoroughly prick the crust all over, up the sides too, with a fork. This will help keep it from shrinking (although it will anyway, so don't worry, it's the sign of a good homemade pie). Bake 10 - 12 min. until golden brown.

# Piecraft

Tender-crisp flaky homemade pie crust, twisted & twirled at the rim truly does make the world a better place. ♥ If you'd like to see someone melt before your very eyes, surprise them with a homemade pie. ♥

THERE'S NOTHING TO IT, YOU JUST DO IT. ♥

✳        ✳        ✳

Pre-baking pastry cut-outs helps keep their shape.

Old-fashioned basket weave.
♥

Rustic-free form. Put pastry circle on cookie sheet & chill. Mound filling in center; fold pastry up & over.

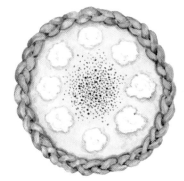

Braid thin strips of dough; adhere with egg wash.

Cookie cutters are so INSPIRING.

Cut shapes into top crust before putting it on. ♥

For a shiny crust, brush it with beaten egg. For matt browning, brush crust with milk. No two pies will ever look alike ~ imperfection is a big part of their charm. ♥

# APPLE CRISP

375° Serves Six

In my humble opinion (oxymoron :) this is the perfect apple crisp—with a thick, crunchy topping. Serve it either hot or cold — pour cream over or serve with ice cream. ♥

About 4 medium, peeled, sliced, tart apples (Granny Smith)
3/4 c. firmly packed brown sugar
½ c. flour
½ c. oats
3/4 tsp. cinnamon
3/4 tsp. nutmeg
1/3 c. softened butter

Preheat oven. Butter a square baking pan. Place the apple slices in pan. Mix remaining ingredients and sprinkle over apples. Bake 30 minutes or until apples are tender and topping is golden brown. ♥

"My garden will never make me famous,
I'm a horticultural ignoramus,
I can't tell a stringbean from a soybean,
Or even a girl bean from a boy bean."
Ogden Nash ♥

# APPLE SEASON

Here in New England we celebrate the arrival of Fall in many ways ~ it's an exhilarating time of change signaled at first by a quick drop in temperature, then a gradual turn of the leaves from their Summer greens to the magnificent golds and reds of Fall. It's a time to prepare for the cold to come, to make the garden secure with rototilling and mulch, to finish the last freezing and canning for the Winter supply, to put the pumpkin on the porch and the wreath of dried flowers on the door. Time for cozy dinners of soup and bread and in door games by a toasty fire. It is also Apple Season 🍎 and is heralded by the many busy roadside stands with their big baskets of juicy apples for sale. I want to give you just a few examples of the different tastes available and some of their uses:

· Granny Smith · Golden Delicious · Cortland · Delicious ·

Tart hard apple ~ use in pies & apple crisp ♥

Sweet, fine-grained, use in salads & for baking ♥

softer sweeter apple ~ use for baked apple ♥

Crispy and juicy ~ coat with caramel for Halloween treats ♥

· McIntosh · Jonathan ·

good eating, wonderful with cheese ♥

Tart and juicy, good for applesauce ♥

126

# BANANA CREAM PIE

*This pie is luscious!*                              *Serves Eight*

½ c. sugar
6 Tbsp. flour
¼ tsp. salt
2½ c. milk
2 egg yolks
1 Tbsp. butter

½ tsp. vanilla extract
3 ripe bananas
1 baked 9" pie shell (p. 129)
½ c. shredded coconut
1½ c. cream, whipped

Mix sugar, flour & salt in the top part of a double boiler. Gradually stir in milk and cook over boiling water ~ stir constantly until thickened. Cover & cook 10 min. longer, stirring occasionally. Beat egg yolks & add to them a small amount of milk mixture. Return mixture to the double boiler & cook for 2 min. over hot, not boiling, water. Stir constantly. Remove from heat ~ stir in butter & extract. Cool. Slice 2 bananas into bottom of pie shell and arrange evenly. Pour cooked mixture over bananas and refrigerate. Spread coconut on a cookie sheet and toast at 350° ~ it burns easily so stir often. Before serving, cover pie with whipped cream, arrange remaining sliced banana around the edge of pie, and put the toasted coconut in the center.

Garden Tip: For bigger, healthier flowers, plant banana skins at the base of your roses.

# BANANA FRITTERS

4-5 Servings

This is a very special dessert, crunchy on the outside, soft in the middle.

1 egg
1/3 c. milk
1/2 c. flour
2 tsp. sugar
1/2 tsp. baking powder
1/2 tsp. salt

2 tsp. melted butter
4 bananas
juice of one lemon
2 Tbsp. powdered sugar
cooking oil
sour cream (or ice cream)

Separate the egg & beat the white until stiff. Beat the yolk with milk. Stir in the flour mixed with sugar, baking powder, and salt. Stir in the melted butter. Fold in beaten egg white. Cut the bananas into chunks and squeeze the lemon juice over them. Sprinkle them with the powdered sugar. Dip the banana pieces into the batter and fry in two inches of hot oil. Top with sour cream or ice cream, and serve immediately.

# BANANA ICE CREAM

Easy, and healthy. Take frozen banana chunks from your freezer, put in blender with milk to cover, add a tsp. of coffee and a tsp. of vanilla. Blend, serve, yum.

# Pink Sugar Frosting

Enough for 24 cupcakes or to fill & frost a three-layer 8" cake.

2 unbeaten egg whites
1½ c. sugar
5 tbsp. cold water

¼ tsp. cream of tartar
1½ tsp. light corn syrup
zest of 1 tangerine (or an orange)
½ tsp. triple sec

Put first 6 ingred. in top of double boiler over boiling water. Beat constantly with electric mixer for 7 min. Remove from stove, add triple sec; continue beating until frosting stands in peaks.

Carefully add a couple of drops of red food coloring to turn the frosting baby pink. (Divide frosting into smaller bowls if you'd like to do other colors.) Decorate with coconut, animal cookies, fresh flowers, chocolate chips, gum drops, crushed peppermint candy, raspberries & mint leaves, or sparkly sprinkles.

## CIRCUS CAKE

This is the method for my mom's Circus Cake, the one that set our young household on fire with anticipation.

Use any cake recipe you like. I decorated mine with coconut, gum drops, animal cookies, & red-&-white striped candles. I used long candles to hold up my "tent"; my mom did hers with peppermint candy sticks & she stuck her candles into Life Savers.

TAKE OFF THE TOP
LIGHT THE CANDLES
CLOSE YOUR EYES
Make a Wish

To make the "tent," draw a 9" circle on the backside of cute scrapbook paper (use a bowl as a template); cut it out, scallop the edges or use pinking shears. Put a pencil dot in the center; cut to the dot; overlap the edges & glue.

# CRÈME CARAMEL

325° Serves Eight

Light, delicate and elegant — also, totally delicious. This is my favorite dessert. ♥ When inverted into serving dish the caramel surrounds the custard like an island. ♥

| | |
|---|---|
| 3 eggs | 1 c. hot cream |
| 2 egg yolks | 1½ tsp. vanilla |
| ½ c. sugar | ♥ ♥ ♥ ♥ |
| 2 c. hot milk | ¾ c. sugar, melted |

Preheat oven to 325°. Beat eggs & yolks together, just to blend. Heat milk and cream together. Stir sugar into eggs; slowly add hot milk & cream, stirring constantly. Add vanilla. To make caramel: Put ¾ c. sugar into dry skillet over medium flame. Swirl pan, but don't stir. Cook till deep caramel color. It dries as it cools, so work quickly. Divide the caramel among 8 buttered ramekins & swirl each. Set the dishes into a roasting pan. Pour boiling water into roasting pan to about 1" deep. Pour the custard into ramekins, filling about ¾ full. Put the roasting pan into oven for 45 min. till a knife, inserted in middle, comes out clean. Cool, then chill, covered in refrigerator. To serve, cut tightly around ramekin — invert small bowl over ramekin — turn both upside-down — pudding will slide out. ♥

# RICE PUDDING

8 Servings

My mother's favorite dessert. I like to serve it with whipped cream or just plain cream poured over the top. It's a comforting type of dessert, good in the wintertime, and not unhealthful. ♥

1 c. arborio rice
6 c. milk (2% is fine)
½ vanilla bean, split & scraped

3 Tbsp. packed brown sugar
½ c. raisins

Rinse rice well & combine with all other ingred. in lg saucepan (split vanilla bean down its length; scrape seeds into pan; add scraped bean to pan.) Bring to boil; reduce heat & simmer, stirring very frequently until rice is tender & liquid is mostly absorbed; 40-45 min. Pudding thickens a bit as it cools. Remove vanilla bean. Serve warm or chilled. Keeps in your fridge up to four days (but good luck with that!).

ONE PINT MILK

# CHOCOLATE SHOT COOKIES

325° Makes 2½ dozen

A buttery cookie made for me every year by my Grandma — and I love them. ♥

1 c. butter
1 c. powdered sugar
2 tsp. vanilla
1½ c. unbleached flour
½ tsp. baking soda
1 c. oatmeal
2 bottles chocolate shots

First off, chocolate shots are those little short chocolate pieces sold in plastic containers in the cake decorating section. ♥ Cream the butter & sugar till fluffy. Add vanilla, flour, soda & oatmeal, mixing thoroughly. Chill for about 2 hours. Shape into 3 rolls (the width of a cookie) & roll in chocolate shots. Slice 3/8" thick & bake on ungreased cookie sheet for 20~25 min. at 325°. ♥ You can freeze the uncooked rolls & slice off as many as you need (in case of surprise visit by Cookie Monster). ♥

Happy and successful cooking doesn't rely only on know-how; it comes from the heart.
♥ George Blanc

# CHOCOLATE MOUSSE PIE

Serves Ten

A chocolate dream in a chocolate cookie crust. ♥

## Crust:

1½ pkgs. chocolate wafer cookies, crushed
1 Tbsp. fresh coffee granules
6 Tbsp. butter, melted (or more)

Combine all ingredients ~ use additional butter if you think it needs it ~ you'll want it to hold together when you cut it. Reserve about 2 Tbsp. for garnish. Press into 9" pie plate.

## Mousse:

1 Tbsp. unflavored gelatin
⅓ c. rum
½ c. sugar
5 eggs, separated
3/4 c. crème de cacao

8 oz. semisweet chocolate
1 Tbsp. instant coffee powder
1/4 c. butter, cut into teaspoonfuls
2 c. heavy cream, whipped
1 c. heavy cream, whipped (garnish)

Combine gelatin & rum in a small bowl. Mix well & set aside. Separate eggs ~ reserve whites. Combine sugar & egg yolks in top part of double boiler; beat 3 min. till thickened. Stir in crème de cacao & set over simmering water, beating constantly till mixture is hot & foamy. Remove from heat; add gelatin mixture; beat for 5-6 min. till mixture is cool; set aside. Melt chocolate very slowly in a heavy saucepan. Stir in instant coffee; remove from heat & beat in butter, 1 tsp. at a time. Very slowly, stir the chocolate into egg mixture; beat until mixture is room temperature. Beat reserved egg whites until stiff; fold them into the whipped cream & then fold all into chocolate mixture. Pour into prepared pie plate & refrigerate at least 4 hours. Garnish with additional whipped cream & reserved cookie crumbs. ♥

# BLUEBERRY
## ANGEL DREAM CAKE

375° Serves 8-10

You need a 10" tube pan.

1 c. + 2 tbsp. cake flour
1½ c. sugar (separated)
1 doz. egg whites - room temp.
(about 1½ c.)
1¼ tsp. cream of tartar

½ tsp. salt
zest of one lemon
1 tsp. vanilla extract
1½ c. fresh or frozen
blueberries (thawed
& drained)
Lemon Glaze

*MAY ALL YOUR DREAMS COME TRUE*

Preheat oven to 375°

Roughly measure-out flour & sift twice; remove excess, sift 3 more times w/ ½ c. sugar & set aside. Put egg whites in a large bowl (save time: buy egg whites at store & measure out 1½ c.) Beat w/ mixer until foamy ~ add cream of tartar & salt & beat until soft peaks form. Gradually add 1 c. sugar; beat until stiff peaks form.

Sift flour mixture over egg whites a little at a time; fold gently along w/ zest. Fold in vanilla & blueberries.

Pour batter into ungreased tube pan; spread evenly with scraper. Break up air pockets by weaving knife through batter. Bake 40 min. until cake springs back when lightly touched. Cool pan upside-down on rack. When completely cool, run a knife around inside edge of pan & turn out onto cake plate. Make Lemon Glaze

When cake is cool, drizzle over a mixture of 1 c. sifted powdered sugar combined w/ 3 tbsp. fresh lemon juice. Cut cake w/ serrated knife.

# THREE-LAYER CARROT CAKE

### 325°

This cake goes together so easily and it has everything: it's very moist, chock-full of nuts and fruit, and it's tall and gorgeous ~ A perfect Birthday Cake.

4 eggs, well beaten
1 c. packed brown sugar
1 c. white sugar
1½ c. vegetable oil
2 c. unbleached flour
2 tsp. baking soda
2 tsp. baking powder

2 tsp. cinnamon
1½ tsp. nutmeg
3 c. finely grated carrots
1 c. coconut
1 8oz. can crushed pineapple
1 c. golden raisins
1 c. walnuts, coarsely chopped

Preheat oven to 325°. Oil 3 8" cake pans. Set out ½ c. butter, & 1 8oz. pkg. cream cheese to soften (for frosting). Put pineapple in sieve to drain. Beat eggs in large bowl. Add sugars and beat till light & fluffy. Add oil & mix well with whisk. Put in the dry ingredients & beat till smooth. Stir in remaining ingredients & pour batter into oiled layer pans. Bake for 40 minutes or until knife comes out clean when inserted in center of cake. Cool slightly and frost.

## Frosting

½ c. butter
8 oz. cream cheese
1 1 lb. box powdered sugar
3 tsp. vanilla

Mix together till smooth. Frost between layers & on top. Try toasted coconut for decoration. ♥

For 15 cupcakes, halve the recipe, fill liners ⅔ full, bake 20 min.

MOM

HER CHILDREN RISE UP AND CALL HER BLESSED

Call your mother. ❤ Your Mother

# PIGGYBACK COOKIES

375° Makes about 6 dozen

This is a cookie made from a cookie! Brilliant concept!
Bendy & chewy & filled with chocolate chips ~ DELICIOUS! ♡

2¾ c. broken gingersnap cookies
½ c. flour
2 tsp. baking powder
1 14-oz. can sweetened
   condensed milk
½ c. butter, softened
1¼ c. shredded coconut (sweet)
1¼ c. chopped walnuts
1 c. chocolate chips

HAVE ONE!

Heat oven to 375°. Into the bowl of a food processor, put the
broken gingersnaps, the flour & baking powder; whirl
until finely ground. In a large bowl, with a hand blender,
beat condensed milk & butter until smooth. Add the
gingersnap mixture to bowl & stir well. Stir in coconut,
chocolate chips, & walnuts. Drop by rounded teaspoonfuls
onto ungreased cookie sheets. Bake 8-10 min., until edges
are lightly brown. Cool on waxed paper; store in air~
tight container. ♥ NOW GO OUTSIDE for A BIG BREATH of FRESH AIR ~
COME BACK IN & SEE HOW GOOD YOUR KITCHEN SMELLS. ♥

What lies behind you & what lies in front of
you pales in comparison to what lies inside of you.
              Ralph Waldo Emerson

# BREAD & BUTTER
## PUDDING
### 350°   Serves Eight

A cozy kind of dessert ~ have it in front of the fireplace when the leaves start to fall. ♥

about ½ loaf French bread
6 Tbsp. unsalted butter, softened
4 eggs
3 egg yolks
2 c. milk
1 c. heavy cream
½ c. sugar
2 tsp. vanilla

Preheat oven to 350°.  Cut crust off of bread & slice ½" thick ~ you'll need 15~20 slices. Butter each slice & overlap them in a buttered 7"×10" baking dish ~ fill dish completely.  Combine eggs & yolks in a large mixing bowl & beat them just to blend. In a saucepan combine milk, cream & sugar over medium high heat; bring to simmer to dissolve sugar. Very slowly, whisking constantly, add the hot milk to the eggs. Add the vanilla & pour over prepared bread slices. Place baking dish in a larger pan, then into oven. Pour about 1" hot water into larger pan (so it surrounds baking dish) & bake 45-50 min., till a knife comes out clean.  Serve hot or cold, plain, or with whipped cream and/or berries. ♥

# CHOCOLATE CREAM PUFFS

375°   Sixteen small puffs

Basic Pastry:
- ♥ ¼ c. butter
- ♥ ½ c. water
- ♥ ½ c. flour
- ♥ 2 eggs, room temp.

Boil the water and butter together in small saucepan. Remove from heat and add flour all at once, beating rapidly till dough leaves the side of the pan and forms a ball. (If it doesn't, put it back on medium heat and keep beating.) Cool for 5 minutes. Add eggs one at a time, beating frantically after each until dough is smooth. Drop small teaspoonfuls on an ungreased cookie sheet 2" apart and bake for about 16 minutes in pre~ heated 375° oven till brown and puffed. Cool. Just before serving, fill with whipped cream by slicing off the very top, & pulling out any wet filaments of dough. Spoon hot chocolate sauce over filled puffs, letting it dribble down the sides.♥

♥ · ♥ · ♥   Chocolate Sauce   ♥ · ♥ · ♥

Over low flame, heat 3 oz. semi~sweet chocolate & 2 Tbsp. butter, stirring constantly. The sauce will thicken as it cools, so spoon it over puffs rather quickly.♥

♥ · ♥ · ♥

For a charming gift, line a pretty box with large paper doilies, and fill the box with cream puffs, each on its own small round doily. Refrigerate until ready to go. ♥

# DEATH BY CHOCOLATE

### 350°  Serves Eight

What a way to go. ♥ Your victim will love you. ♥ A chocolaty ice cream cake roll finished off with a dollop of thick fudgy killer chocolate sauce. ♥

¼ c. cocoa

1¼ c. powdered sugar

5 eggs

1 tsp. vanilla

¼ tsp. salt

1 qt. good vanilla ice cream

Preheat oven to 350°. Sift cocoa & sugar together. Separate the eggs; put the yolks & vanilla in a large bowl & beat very well until thick. In another bowl whisk the egg whites till foamy; add salt & continue beating till soft peaks are formed. Fold the cocoa & sugar into the whites, then gently fold ⅓ of egg white mixture into the beaten yolks. Thoroughly butter a 10"×15" cookie sheet & line it with wax paper. Spread the batter evenly in the pan; bake 18~20 min., until knife comes out clean. Sprinkle a clean tea towel with powdered sugar & turn cake out onto it. Remove wax paper & trim off any crispy edges. Roll the cake in the towel from the long end [ ↑ ] & let it rest 1-2 min. Unroll & let it rest again for a few min., then roll it up again & allow it to cool completely. Set ice cream out to soften. Unroll the cooled cake; spread evenly with ice cream & roll it back up (without the tea towel). Dust the top with powdered sugar. Keep it in the freezer till ready to serve. When ready, cut the cake & serve it with the hot chocolate sauce on the side. ♥

## Killer Chocolate Sauce

3 Tbsp. unsalted butter

4 oz. unsweetened chocolate

2/3 c. boiling water

1½ c. sugar

7 Tbsp. corn syrup

1 tsp. vanilla

Melt the butter & chocolate in a heavy saucepan over low heat; add boiling water & stir well. Mix in the sugar & corn syrup ~till sauce is smooth. Boil the sauce, without stirring, for 10 min.; remove from heat; cool 20 min., then add the vanilla. Spoon the sauce over the ice cream cake and serve. ♥

# CRANBERRY TEA CAKE

### 350° Serves 12

Jewel-like cranberries & sticky toasted pecans; serve it for holiday breakfast, at a tea party, or for a summer brunch. So easy to make; goes together quickly. ♥

½ stick butter (4 tbsp.)
1 c. dark brown sugar
½ c. whole raw pecans
3 c. fresh or thawed
   whole cranberries
3 eggs
1 c. sugar
1½ c. sifted flour

½ tsp. baking powder
½ tsp. salt
zest of 1 lg. orange
½ c. orange juice
   (about 1½ lg. oranges)
1½ tsp. vanilla

### Vanilla Sauce
(NEXT PAGE)

Preheat oven to 350°. Melt butter in 9" cake pan; swirl to distribute. Sprinkle brown sugar evenly over the butter. Arrange a row of whole pecans around the outside of the pan. Coarsely chop remaining nuts & sprinkle over center of cake pan. Pour over cranberries & distribute evenly. Put pan in oven to warm while you make the batter.

In a med. bowl, beat eggs until foamy; gradually beat in sugar. Add orange zest, juice, & vanilla. Sift & measure flour, add baking powder & salt to it. Add dry ingredients, all at once, to batter & beat smooth. Slowly pour batter over cranberries. Bake 45-50 min. until a skewer, stuck in the center of cake, comes out clean. Run a knife around outside edge of cake; turn out immediately; here's how: Set a large cake plate upside-down on the pan & flip over, both together. Cool.

# Vanilla Sauce

1" piece vanilla bean          1/4 c. sugar
2 c. heavy cream

While cake is baking, make the sauce. Slit vanilla bean in half & scrape pulp into small saucepan. Discard pod (or put it in your sugar bowl for vanilla-flavored sugar). Stir in cream & bring to boil. Add sugar; stir & let cool. Chill well.

To serve, cake should be warm or at room temp. Put a slice of cake in a puddle of chilled sauce. ♥

The only real stumbling block is fear of failure. In cooking you've got to have a what-the-hell attitude.
♥ Julia Child

PICK YOURSELF UP, DUST YOURSELF OFF, & START ALL OVER AGAIN.

## Shocking New Recipe

Tisbury firefighters came to the aid of cookbook author Susan Branch Friday morning after an electrical short in the clock of her stove caused some sparks, smoke, and not much more in the way of damage.

Tisbury fire chief Richard Clark noted, "I guess she was working on a shocking new cake recipe."

← This would look a lot nicer if it hadn't spent several years hanging on our fridge. ♥

OUR FIRE CHIEF SHOULD BE A STAND-UP COMEDIAN. ♥

145

## ICE CREAM SANDWICHES
# FIRECRACKERS

Don't be frightened by the ingredients, these are firecrackers for the mouth, sparklers for the tastebuds, good enough to serve at a dinner party, or eat them barefooted, leaning against your kitchen counter on a summer day.

BRING THEM TO A SUMMER PARTY

or book club ♥

2 boxes (in case some are broken) very thin vanilla-flavored, flower-shaped wafer cookies
1 pint coconut-pineapple ice cream (vanilla works, too)
Freshly ground black pepper, large grind
1 jar pickled ginger (the kind you get with sushi)
whole basil leaves (opt.)

Put cookie sheet or a plate in the freezer. Use a wide knife or a spreader to cut into ice cream to make a 3/4" patty about same size as cookie. Place patty on underside of cookie & mold gently with thumbs. Grind over pepper, then top w/3 pieces ginger. Add basil leaf. Add a small dot of ice cream & stick the top cookie to it, pretty-side-up, pressing down gently. As each is done, put into freezer. When frozen, stack them into a smaller bowl & cover w/plastic wrap until serving time. ♥

# Kewpie Dolls

Use Nabisco Famous Chocolate Wafers to make these in all colors & flavors. Make the ice cream patties as above — from pistachio, orange & raspberry sherbet, strawberry, mint chocolate chip & coffee ice cream. You can roll the edges in colored candies, toasted coconut, fresh coffee grounds, or chocolate shots. Keep them in the freezer for summer treats ♥.

# Basil Ice Cream

## WITH Summer Tomatoes

### 1 Quart = 8 servings

Yesterday, three girlfriends came to a kitchen-table tea. I served lavender Earl Grey tea & this amazing dessert with basil & tomatoes from our garden. AWESOME in the truest sense of the word. Easy too!

**ICE CREAM:**

3 c. heavy cream
1 c. milk
1/3 c. sugar
1 c. packed basil leaves
6 egg yolks, room temp.
1 lemon; juice & zest

**EVERYTHING ELSE YOU NEED:**

Garden-grown tomatoes, 1/2 c. per serving
salt & freshly-ground pepper
olive oil
Balsamic Syrup (BELOW)

Put cream, milk & 1/2 c. basil in a lg. saucepan; bring to boil, cover, & let stand for 1 hr. Add sugar; stir to dissolve. Return liquid to boil. Whisking constantly, add hot liquid in thin, intermittent stream to egg yolks until yolks are hot, return all to pan. Beat over low heat until thickened (4 or 5 min.). Chill overnight.

Put mixture in blender w/ remaining basil, zest, & juice; blend until smooth. Spin in ice cream machine, then put into container & freeze at least 4 hrs. Make:

## BALSAMIC SYRUP: Boil 1 c. balsamic vinegar; watch carefully until it's reduced to a syrup. Chill.

## TO SERVE: Put about 1/2 c. chopped tomato per serving in a bowl. Sprinkle over salt & pepper; stir in a splash of olive oil. Cuddle ice cream next to a scoop of tomatoes & drizzle w/ about 1/2 tbsp. of syrup. Serve.

# WINTER WARMERS

## IRISH COFFEE

For each drink... **P**ut 1½ oz. Irish Whiskey in a tempered glass or mug; add ½ oz. Kahlua or Baileys; fill with hot coffee & stir in a spoonful of sugar. Float a generous scoop of whipped cream on top & drizzle with a little creme de menthe. Serve with a spoon.

LEPRECHAUNS LEAVE GOLD (FOIL-WRAPPED) CHOCOLATE COINS UNDER PILLOWS, IN SOCK DRAWERS, IN BACK-PACKS, POCKETS & PURSES, CREATING MYSTERY.

**O**nly Irish coffee provides in a single glass all four essential food groups: alcohol, caffein, sugar & fat.
♥ Alex Levine

## DESSERT CHOCOLATE
### LIQUID HAPPINESS

4 servings in mugs ♥          10 servings in demitasse ♥

Rich delicious hot chocolate ~ a very special ending to a meal.

| | |
|---|---|
| 4 oz. semi~sweet chocolate | 1 c. heavy cream, whipped |
| ⅓ c. sugar | Peppermint Schnapps (opt.) |
| 1¼ c. boiling water | fresh coffee grains (opt.) |
| 4 c. very hot milk | cocoa powder (opt.) |
| 1 tsp. vanilla | cinnamon stick swizzles (opt.) |

Melt the chocolate in double boiler ~ stir in the sugar, then slowly add boiling water, whisking well. Stir in the very hot milk. Simmer about 7~8 min. Beat very well until frothy; stir in vanilla. ♥ If using demi-tasse, put about 1 tbsp. Peppermint Schnapps in each cup. Fill with hot chocolate ~ add a dollop of whipped cream & a sprinkle of either coffee grains or cocoa powder & serve. ♥ If using mugs, put a shot of Schnapps in each mug; fill with chocolate; top with whipped cream. Sprinkle on cocoa or coffee grains ~ add a cinnamon stick to each mug & serve. ♥

# SUMMER COOLERS
## Pink Grapefruit Splash

MAKES 1 LG. (16 OZ.) ICE TEA GLASSFUL

Fill glass 2/3 full w/ crushed ice
Pour over: 1/2 c. fresh-squeezed grapefruit juice
      3/4 c. tonic
      1/4 c. gin (or rum, both good; this is also
         good without alcohol!)
Garnish w/ lime squeeze or a slice of
green apple.    FYI: FOUR SQUEEZED

GRAPEFRUITS = APPROX. 2 1/2 C. JUICE.

# BASIL LIMEADE
## PITCHER - PERFECT

1/2 c. sugar + 1 c. water
4 whole basil leaves
4 limes, quartered
1/4 c. sweetened, con-
   densed milk
4 c. cold water
GARNISH WITH basil or
      mint.

Put sugar & water in a small saucepan & bring to boil. Remove from heat, stir in basil & chill. When cold, pour it into blender w/ limes, condensed milk & 2 c. cold water. Blend 4 seconds on high.

Strain into pitcher. Rinse blender w/ 2 c. cold water, pour it through remains in strainer into pitcher (to get rest of juice). Pour into glasses over crushed ice, garnish & welcome to happy town.

"Stands the church clock at ten to three?
And is there honey still for tea?"
Rupert Brooke

# BREAKFAST

"You have to eat oatmeal or you'll
dry up. Anybody knows that."
_Eloise_ ♥ Kay Thompson ♥

# ❤ • ❤ BREAKFAST ❤ • ❤

Breakfast! My favorite meal ~ you can be so creative. I think of bowls of sparkling berries and fresh cream, baskets of ♫ Popovers and Croissants ♪ with little pots of jams and jellies, steaming coffee and freshly squeezed orange juice, thick country bacon, hot maple syrup, pancakes and French toast ~ even the nutty flavor of Irish Oatmeal with brown sugar and cream. ❤ Breakfast is the place I splurge with calories, then I spend the rest of the day getting ♪ them off! I love to use my prettiest table settings ~ crocheted placemats with lace-edged napkins and old hammered silver. And whether you are inside in front of a fire, candles burning brightly on a wintery day ~ or outside on a patio enjoying the morning sun ~ whether you are having a group of friends and family, ♫ a quiet little brunch for two, or an even quieter little brunch just for yourself ❤, breakfast can set the mood and pace of the whole day.

♪ And Sunday is my day. ❤ Sometimes I think we get caught up in the hectic happenings of the weeks and months and ♫ we forget to take time out to relax. So one snowy Sunday I decided to do things differently ~ now ♪ it's gotten to be a sort of ritual! This is what I do: at around 8:30 am. I pull myself from my warm cocoon, fluff up the pillows and blankets and put some classical music on the stereo. ❤ Then I'm off to the kitchen, where I very calmly (so as not to wake myself up too much!) prepare my breakfast, ♪ something extra nice ~ last week I had fresh pineapple slices wrapped in bacon and broiled, a warm croissant, hot chocolate with marshmallows & orange juice. I put ♪ it all on a tray with a cloth napkin, my book-of-the-moment and the "Travel" section of the Boston Globe and take it back to bed with me. There I ♪ ♪ spend the next 2 hours reading, eating and dreaming ❤ while the snowflakes swirl through the treetops outside my bedroom

❤ ❤ ❤ ❤ ❤

window. ♫ The inspiring music of Bach or Vivaldi adds an exquisite elegance to the otherwise unruly scene, and I am in heaven. ♥ I found time to get in touch with myself and my life ♪ and I think this just might be a necessity! Please try it for yourself, and someone you love. ♥

# BEST BISCUITS

425° Makes about 14

Hot, flaky, melt-in-your-mouth biscuits ~ for breakfast! Best served with honey butter: a mixture of softened butter and honey to taste. ♥ Don't forget these for your Sunday chicken dinners. ♥ And one more idea: chop fresh strawberries & heat them with a tiny bit of sugar to taste. Pour the berries over hot, split biscuits ~ finish with a big dollop of sweetened whipped cream. ♥

2 c. unbleached flour
1 Tbsp. baking powder
1¼ tsp. salt

2½ tsp. sugar
1½ c. heavy cream
4 Tbsp. melted butter

Preheat oven to 425°. Put flour, baking powder, salt & sugar into mixing bowl ~ stir with fork. Slowly add 1 to 1½ c. cream, stirring constantly, just until dough comes together. Place dough on floured board & knead for 1 minute. Pat dough flat to about ¾" thick. Cut with round 2" cookie cutter & brush both sides with melted butter. Place the buttered biscuits 1" apart on ungreased cookie sheet. Bake 15~18 min., till browned. Wrap them in a napkin & serve them in a basket. ♥

154

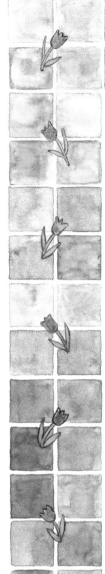

# APPLESAUCE

Makes 4 cups

Make your own applesauce, and it won't be the smoothed~out kind you get at the market. I like to serve it hot at breakfast with Popovers (p.165) or German Pancake (p.162) or Cottage Cheese Pancakes (p.163). Also very good with Veal Birds (p.92). I make it and put it up in jars and give it away at Christmastime. ♥

4 med. tart apples, peeled, cored & quartered
1 c. water
½ c. brown sugar
¼ tsp. cinnamon
⅛ tsp. nutmeg
1 Tbsp. butter
¾ c. chopped walnuts (opt.)
½ c. raisins, golden kind (opt.)
⅓ c. coconut (opt.)

Put the apples & water in a pot and heat over medium heat until boiling. Reduce to simmer and stir occasionally for 5 to 10 minutes until apples are tender. Add all the other ingredients and heat through until raisins are plumped. ♥

♥ ♥ ♥ ♥ ♥ ♥ ♥

# CORNMEAL MUFFINS

375° Makes 1 dozen

For this recipe I love to use my cast iron muffin pans that symbolize the four seasons. Folklore says that the heart shape is for spring, the round cup for the summer sun, the scalloped cup for the fall foliage and the star stands for the winter sky. The cups are shallow so the muffins come out extra crisp and light. When using this type of pan, fill the cups full, but when using a regular muffin pan, only fill it ²/₃ full. ♥

½ c. yellow cornmeal
½ c. unbleached flour
2 tsp. baking powder
1½ tsp. sugar
1 tsp. salt

½ tsp. cinnamon
1 egg
3/4 c. milk
2 Tbsp. melted butter
Honey butter

Preheat oven to 375° Sift all dry ingredients into a bowl. Mix liquids together, then combine with dry ingredients. Pour batter into well~buttered muffin pans and bake for 20 min. until lightly browned. Serve with honey butter: cream softened butter with honey to taste. ♥

# CRISPY
# POTATO PANCAKES

Serves Six

Brown and crispy, these are great with sausages and homemade applesauce (p.155) for breakfast. ♥

4 large russet potatoes
1 egg, beaten
1½ Tbsp. flour
2 Tbsp. cream
salt & pepper to taste
oil for frying

Peel the potatoes and grate them. Put them in a large tea towel & twist to remove moisture. Immediately put the potatoes into a bowl with beaten egg, flour, cream, and salt & pepper. (The potatoes will turn brown if not cooked immediately after grating.) Mix well. Heat oil in large skillet. Put a couple of spoonfuls into the hot oil and mash with spatula to form a pancake. Cook them over moderate heat till browned on both sides. Put them in a warm oven till they're all cooked. Serve hot. ♥

# OATMEAL
## BREAKFAST OF CHAMPIONS

## Muesli

Served ice cold, the oats stay a little crunchy. For each serving, put about ¼ c. of slow-cooking, Quaker oats (uncooked) in a cereal bowl. Sprinkle with cinnamon, chopped walnuts, & raisins. Cover w/milk. Stir, cover, & refrigerate at least 1 hr. (or overnight). Delicious as is, or gild the lily w/chopped apple.

## STEEL-CUT
## Irish Oatmeal

~ Steel-cut Irish oats ~
I ♥ McCanns; available in grocery stores.
~ Fresh or frozen organic blueberries

~ chopped walnuts
~ cinnamon
~ brown sugar (opt.)
~ milk

Make oatmeal according to package. Sprinkle with blueberries, walnuts, cinnamon, & brown sugar (if you like). Pour over milk & enjoy.

Bought MARMALADE? OH DEAR, I CALL THAT VERY FEEBLE. ♥ Julian Fellowes

# Cranberry Marmalade

350°

I discovered this by accident one Christmas with some left-over cranberry sauce ~ so good, now I make it on purpose. Beyond easy; such a pretty gift; make extra for a friend. ♥ Amazing on hot, buttered biscuits (p. 154).

1 c. fresh or frozen cranberries
1/3 c. sugar
1 c. good-quality orange marmalade

Preheat oven to 350°

Put cranberries into a small ungreased baking dish. Sprinkle over sugar; don't stir. Put into oven (stir 3 times during baking); bake 30-35 minutes, until berries begin to pop. Remove from oven & cool. Combine cranberries with the orange marmalade & chill. Here's what to do with it: make toast with good sour dough bread. Spread it with butter & lather on the marmalade. Note the berry round-ness on the toast? Bite it. Yuuuum. Try it on English muffins; cream scones for tea; or on fresh baked biscuits with a roasted chicken dinner.

Vintage coasters make perfect jam-jar toppers. Secure with rubber band; cover it with a ribbon. ♥

# ❖ GERMAN PANCAKE ❖

450° Serves Four

This pancake puffs up over the top of the pan ~ it has an eggy~soft middle and is browned and crusty on the outside. For a sumptuous brunch serve it with fat sausages, baked bananas with vanilla ice cream, watermelon balls and champagne. ♥

4 eggs
2/3 c. flour
1 tsp. salt
2/3 c. milk
3 Tbsp. butter

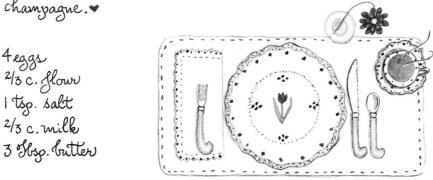

Butter a heavy 10" oven-proof skillet. Preheat oven to 450°. Beat the eggs with a fork to blend. Slowly add flour, beating constantly. Stir in salt & milk. Pour the batter into the skillet & drop the butter by teaspoonfuls into the batter, spreading evenly. Bake at 450° for 15 minutes ~ reduce heat to 350° and bake another 10 minutes. Remove from oven and sift powdered sugar over the top. Serve with heated maple syrup. ♥

To bake bananas: Put one ripe banana per serving on a cookie sheet (in its skin). Bake at 350° until it turns completely black, about 20 minutes. Slit open & moosh up, same as you would with a baked potato. Delicious with vanilla ice cream and a sprinkle of fresh coffee grounds. ♥

# COTTAGE CHEESE PANCAKES

Makes 8 Pancakes

These pancakes are healthier, have more texture, & taste better than normal pancakes. Serve them with hot Applesauce (p.155) and Banana Fritters with ice cream (p. 124) for a warming winter breakfast feast. ♥

1 c. cottage cheese, drained
3 eggs
¼ c. flour (gluten free, if you like)

2 Tbsp. melted butter
¼ tsp. cinnamon
¼ tsp. salt

Squeeze the cottage cheese dry in a piece of cheesecloth. Beat the eggs in a mixing bowl; add the cottage cheese & all other ingredients — mix just to blend. Drop by large spoonfuls into buttered & oiled moderately hot skillet. Cook fairly slowly until brown on both sides. Keep them warm in a 200° oven till all are done. Serve with heated Vermont maple syrup. ♥

"The wind was blowing, but not too hard, and everyone was so happy and gay for it was only twenty degrees below zero and the sun shone."
♥ Laura Ingalls Wilder ♥

# Blueberry Corncakes

Serves 4

Crisp on the edges with a cornmeal crunch in the tender middle. Perfect for a winter day.

2/3 c. flour
1/2 c. yellow cornmeal
3 Tbsp. sugar
1 Tbsp. baking powder
2 tsp. cinnamon
1/4 tsp. salt

1 egg
1 c. milk
2 Tbsp. canola oil
1 c. blueberries,
fresh or frozen
(not thawed)

In a lg. bowl, whisk together first six ingred. In another bowl, whisk egg well; whisk in milk, then canola oil. Pour into dry ingred. & stir until just blended. Gently fold in blueberries. Heat skillet with 1 Tbsp. each canola oil & butter. Drop batter by spoonfuls into pan; use back of spoon to spread batter into 4" rounds. When crisp & brown, turn & do other side. Keep warm in 250° oven. Serve in a puddle of hot maple syrup — butter is optional. ♥ You will be FORTIFIED & can now go out & PLAY IN THE SNOW...

Pure Maple Syrup

IT SNOWED LAST YEAR TOO: I MADE A SNOWMAN & MY BROTHER KNOCKED IT DOWN & I KNOCKED MY BROTHER DOWN & THEN WE HAD TEA.
♥ Dylan Thomas

# POPOVERS

400° Makes 12

These will pop up and over the top of the muffin pan ~ Serve them with marmalade and jam. ♥

3 eggs
1½ c. milk
1 Tbsp. melted butter
1 tsp. salt
1½ c. unbleached flour

Butter 12 cups in muffin pans. Beat all ingredients together until smooth. Fill muffin pans ⅔ full. Bake at 400° for 45 minutes. Take them out and slit the tops ~ return to the oven for 5~10 minutes. Serve them in a large basket wrapped in a pretty cloth. ♥

# BREAKFAST CRÊPES
### Makes 12 crêpes

Crêpes are very easy & kind of fun to make. ♥ I usually triple this recipe & stack them with waxed paper in between & then freeze them. There are lots of ways to use them. ♥

2 eggs, beaten well
1 c. milk
1 c. unbleached flour

1½ Tbsp. butter, melted
½ tsp. vanilla (opt.)
pinch of salt

Add milk to beaten eggs—whisk in all other ingredients; mix till smooth. Lightly oil a 7" skillet (Teflon works great); heat pan till moderately hot. Using a small measuring cup, pour about 3 Tbsp. batter into pan & quickly swirl to coat the bottom (like a very thin pancake). Brown lightly & turn to cook other side. Remove to plate. Finish all & fill with:

## Ricotta Filling
### Serves Six ♥ (2 crêpes each)

Mix together 1 lb. Ricotta cheese, 1 beaten egg, 3 Tbsp. powdered sugar & 2 tsp. lemon zest. Roll into crêpes, dust with powdered sugar & sprinkle over chopped fresh strawberries ~ serve. ♥ ♥ Apple topping for Ricotta-filled crêpes: Put peeled chopped apples in skillet with a little butter. Add brown sugar, chopped walnuts, & a little cinnamon to taste ~ cook till apples soften & pour over filled crêpes. ♥ Crêpes Chantilly: Mix 1 thinly sliced banana with 1 c. whipped cream, 2 Tbsp. powdered sugar & ½ tsp. vanilla. Fill crêpes; top with more sliced banana; sprinkle on some toasted almonds & serve. ♥

# BEER BREAD

### 350°  Makes 1 loaf

Imagine . . . fresh bread in a matter of minutes! Good bread too & healthy. ♥ Makes delicious toast. ♥

1 12 oz. can of beer
¼ c. maple syrup
3 Tbsp. caraway seeds
2 c. whole wheat flour
1 c. unbleached flour
4 Tbsp. baking powder
1 tsp. salt

Preheat oven to 350°. In a small saucepan warm up the beer, maple syrup & caraway seeds. Mix together remaining ingredients, pour warm liquid into flour mixture & mix it up quickly. Pour batter into well-buttered loaf pan. Bake 30 min. ♥  You can also use buttered muffin tins for crusty rolls. Bake for 15 min. ♥

" He drew a circle that shut me out —
Heretic, rebel, a thing to flout.
But Love and I had the wit to win:
We drew a circle that took him in."
♥ Edwin Markham ♥

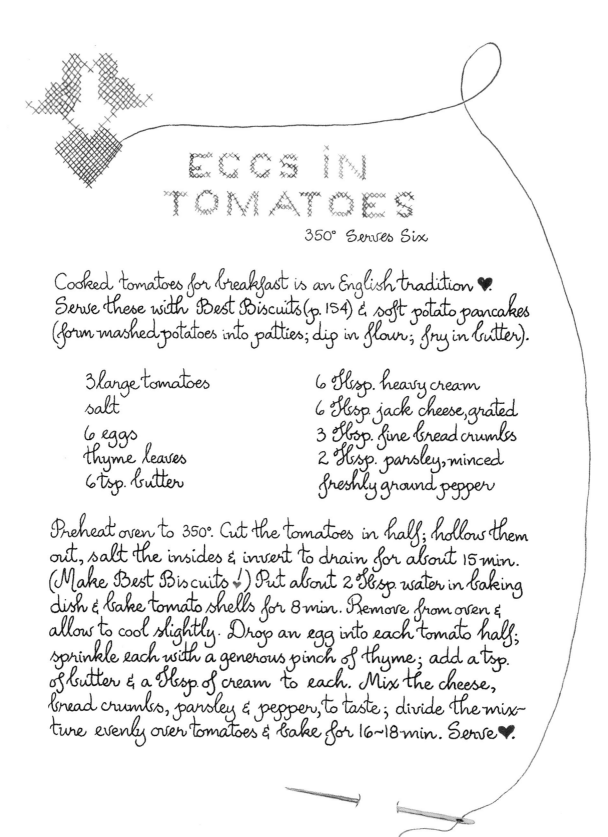

# EGGS IN TOMATOES

350° Serves Six

Cooked tomatoes for breakfast is an English tradition ♥.
Serve these with Best Biscuits (p. 154) & soft potato pancakes
(form mashed potatoes into patties; dip in flour; fry in butter).

3 large tomatoes
salt
6 eggs
thyme leaves
6 tsp. butter

6 Tbsp. heavy cream
6 Tbsp. jack cheese, grated
3 Tbsp. fine bread crumbs
2 Tbsp. parsley, minced
freshly ground pepper

Preheat oven to 350°. Cut the tomatoes in half; hollow them
out, salt the insides & invert to drain for about 15 min.
(Make Best Biscuits!) Put about 2 Tbsp. water in baking
dish & bake tomato shells for 8 min. Remove from oven &
allow to cool slightly. Drop an egg into each tomato half;
sprinkle each with a generous pinch of thyme; add a tsp.
of butter & a Tbsp. of cream to each. Mix the cheese,
bread crumbs, parsley & pepper, to taste; divide the mixture evenly over tomatoes & bake for 16~18 min. Serve ♥.

168

# BREAKFAST · IDEAS

♥ The "Come as you are" party: This was something my parents did during the summers when I was a child & I re-member them because they were so much fun. We have wonderful photos of these parties ~ adults & children all in their pajamas out in our backyard playing croquet, eating a barbecued breakfast, enjoying the early morning sunshine ~ a (planned) spur-of-the-moment party. Secrecy is the key to success. Plan the party ~ make a few loose ground rules about "acceptable party clothes" & simply go to your guests' homes at 7am. on a warm Saturday morning & start rounding them up. After the shock wears off, you'll have a memorable party. ♥

♥ Breakfast hors d'oeuvres: wrap fresh pineapple slices in half-cooked bacon ~ before serving, put them under the broiler to finish the bacon. ♥ Hot Cornmeal Muffins (p.156) served with honey butter. ♥ Fill triangles of Phyllo with a mixture of Ricotta cheese, powdered sugar & lemon zest. Fry quickly in hot butter & oil ~ Sift over a bit more powdered sugar & serve. ♥ Dip large cold strawberries in Chocolate Sauce (p.142) ~ or serve fresh strawberries with a bowl of sweetened whipped cream for dipping. ♥ Make French toast out of cinnamon swirl bread ~ put orange marmalade between the slices; cut into bite-sized pieces. Serve them with yogurt mixed with brown sugar for dipping. ♥ Put watermelon balls on toothpicks; mix sour cream & brown sugar for dipping. ♥

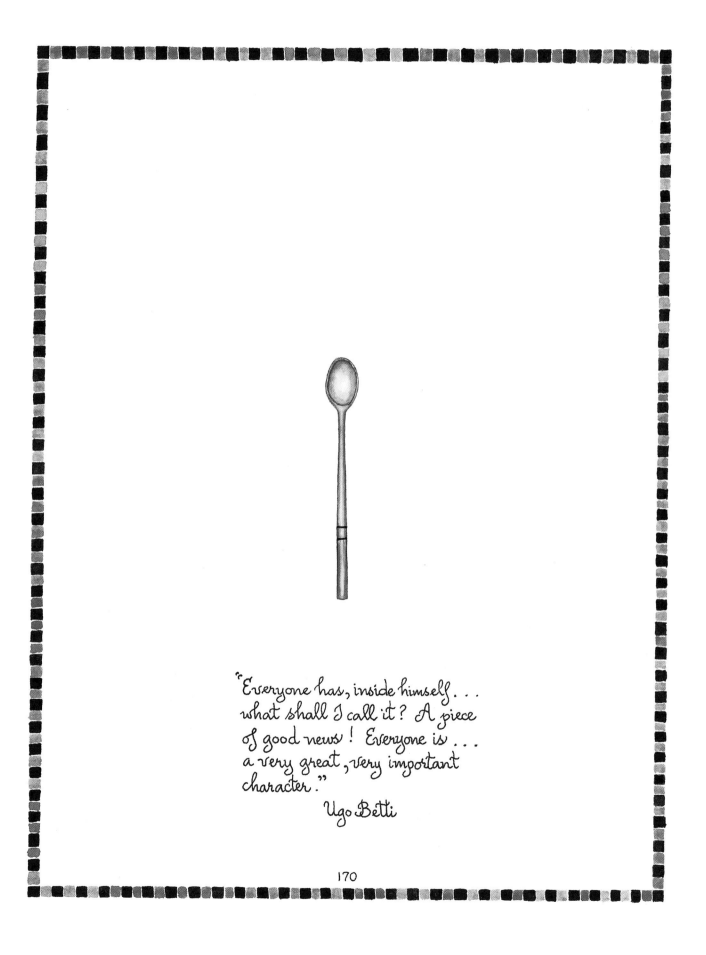

"Everyone has, inside himself . . .
what shall I call it? A piece
of good news! Everyone is . . .
a very great, very important
character."

Ugo Betti

"FRIENDS ~

They are kind
to each other's
HOPES.

They cherish
each other's
DREAMS."

Thoreau

My heartfelt thanks & gratitude for the special en-
couragement from Stan Hart, Jane Bay & Cliff
Branch. ♥ To Diana, the Tuesday Girls, & the
good people at Little, Brown & Company— thank you!
♥ Special thanks to Sandy Haeger, who took
the time to help me.

"A" is for Apple(s) . . .

# INDEX

*Love*

"The sweetest flower that blows, I give you as we part.
For you it is a rose For me it is my heart."
♥ Frederick Peterson

The ordinary arts
we practice every day
at home are of more
importance to the soul
than their simplicity
might suggest.
♥ Thomas Moore

## EVERYDAY KITCHEN HINTS

Soak starchy, eggy, or cheesy pots & pans in cold water for easy clean up.

Too much salt in your soup or stew? Add large slices of raw potato — cook 10 min. Remove potato before serving.

Store leftover avocado in fridge with seed IN.

Always TEAR greens — don't cut, for fresh, wilt-free salads.

Walnuts or pecans, toasted in butter & garlic, are delicious in green salads. For Fall, add dried cranberries, sliced pears, pomegranate seeds, lemon or orange zest.

### YOUR BASIC TABLESETTING

BREAD · WATER · WINE · SALAD · DINNER · DINNER · TEA · SOUP

## PORTION CONTROL

SERVING SIZES CAN BE CONFUSING, SO WHEN YOU HEAR THAT YOU SHOULD HAVE 2-3 "SERVINGS" OF CERTAIN FOODS EACH DAY, HERE'S WHAT IT MEANS:

A 3 oz. SERVING OF FISH OR MEAT IS THE SIZE OF A DECK OF CARDS.

A SERVING SIZE OF FRUIT IS THE SIZE OF A TENNIS BALL.

SHOP FOR THE SMALLER PORTIONS.

½ CUP = 1 SERVING VEGETABLE

A LITTLE PAIR OF DICE EQUALS ONE OZ. CHEESE

A "MED." BAKED POTATO IS ABOUT THE SAME SIZE AS A COMPUTER MOUSE.

THINK A WEIGHT LOSS OF ¼ lb. ISN'T MUCH? IMAGINE A STICK-OF-BUTTER-SIZED-BIT OFF YOU!

A 1-lb.-A-WEEK WEIGHT LOSS IS SAFE & EASY & MORE LIKELY TO STAY OFF. AND, IN ONE YEAR, THAT'S 52 lbs!

BUT WHO'S COUNTING?